BUSINESS WRITING

The Good, the Bad, and the Ugly

MATTHEW SPENCE

BUSINESS WRITING

The Good, the Bad, and the Ugly

A Supplement to

ORGANIZING IDEAS

THE QUIMBY STREET PRESS

The Quimby Street Press
Portland, Oregon
Telephone (503) 224-9168

Manufactured in the United States of America

ISBN-13: 978-1495932892

ISBN-10: 1495932893

Contents

Preface

*B*USINESS WRITING: THE GOOD, THE BAD, AND THE UGLY IS A collection of examples of business writing. It is a companion volume to *Organizing Ideas: The Key to Effective Communication. Business Writing* illustrates the application of the principles of effective writing that are explained in *Organizing Ideas,* and the many uses of the *Worksheet for Organizing Ideas.*

Business writing is most effective when it takes a Position—that is to say, when it advocates a decision or presents the reader with the basis for making a decision. In the *Spence & Company* approach to business writing, we refer to such a document as a "decision-oriented communication."

The purpose in this book is to illustrate how the structure of a document is fundamental to the clarity of its message. You will notice throughout that the clarity of any document can be significantly improved simply by changing the order in which the information is presented.

The book also provides models of standard types of business writing for you to consult when composing particular types of documents.

The examples in this book have been collected from thousands of men and women who have attended *Spence & Company* workshops on business and technical writing. The examples are all authentic. Although the writing style or word choice in many instances may not be mine, or yours for that matter, no changes other than those necessary to protect confidentiality have been made to the manner in which the authors have expressed themselves.

Throughout the book, documents received from clients have been revised to illustrate the principles of effective writing. Original documents are distinguished from their revisions by an icon in the upper right-hand corner—a "Don't do this" symbol for originals and a checkmark for revisions.

1. E-mail: Four Errors to Avoid

THE MOST CONVINCING PROOF OF THE IMPORTANCE OF structure in business writing is a comparison between a muddled mystery story and a well-organized revision.

In this chapter and the next you will see examples of weak documents, drawn from a variety of professions. The present chapter addresses common practices in e-mail writing and ways to improve the effectiveness of e-mail communication. The following chapter will look at how to improve communication in longer, more formal memos.

In both chapters, the examples have most of the ingredients of a complete communication, but in each instance they fail to get the Position across clearly and convincingly. Each example is accompanied by a brief discussion of its shortcomings. The information is then reorganized, sometimes by outlining the document on an *E-mail Outline* or a *Worksheet for Organizing Ideas*, sometimes by simply editing the original version. Finally, you will see a revised version of the same information.

The common approach to composing e-mail is to figure out what you want to say as you write. As a result, we frequently:

1. Fail to make our Position clear.

2. Write our message as a single block of text, without separating each element of the message into a discrete paragraph.

3. Present our ideas in the order in which we did our thinking.

4. Tell a story in which facts or events are presented in chronological order.

In virtually every case, the e-mail is a Mystery Story—only telling readers what we want them to do or believe at the end, if at all.

The "figure it out as I go along" and the Mystery Story approaches account for most of what makes so many e-mails a chore to read and understand, and why some are simply incomprehensible. Avoid these practices and you will not only do your readers a service—you are more likely to get the information or action you need in response to your communication.

An E-mail without a Position

Let's start by looking at an e-mail that illustrates the most common characteristic of poor communication: the absence of a Position. In the e-mail below, what does the writer want the reader to do or believe? The closest this e-mail gets to providing a basis for the reader to make a decision is the comment in the last paragraph that Calloway will get a payback on the cost of purging the duplicate names.

Of course, the shortcomings of this e-mail may result from vague instructions from the reader, such as "Check into the duplicate names problem" as opposed to "Investigate this problem and let me know your thoughts on how it can be corrected." In this case, if the writer had included a thorough account of What Prompts Your Document Now, we'd have a better idea of whom to blame.

You will also note that the subject is just a file reference and the closing sentence of the email has that worn-out phrase "Please do not hesitate. . . ."

Subject: Duplicate Names in Promotional Database

I have audited the promotional database and found that there are approximately 70,000 duplicate names in the file.

Duplicate names result in extra costs to Calloway Computer. These include costs in the form of extra postage and the costs of creating more mail pieces than necessary.

There is also an intangible cost to Calloway that manifests itself in the form of lost reputation. Consumers who receive duplicate mailings may question Calloway's business and computing savvy.

Since mailing 70,000 extra pieces in a promotion would cost at least $37,000, approximately the cost of a purge of the duplicate names in the database, Calloway would break even on the first mailing. Thereafter, we would save money on all future mailings since these extra 70,000 names would no longer exist in the database.

If you have any questions, please do not hesitate to call or e-mail me.

On the next page the information in the e-mail has been mapped onto the *Outline for E-mail and Texting*. Viewed in this way, the writer's objective becomes more evident. Now, it's easier to reformulate the e-mail with a Position that calls for action.

OUTLINE *for* E-MAIL *and* TEXTING

Subject: <u>*Purge of Promotional Database – Recommended*</u>

What prompts your e-mail? <u>*As requested, I audited promotional database: approximately*</u>
<u>*70,000 duplicate names in the file.*</u>

What do you want your reader to do or believe? <u>*Request authorization to purge duplicate*</u>
<u>*names.*</u>

Why? What are your reasons or points? <u>*Purge will pay for itself. Calloway Computer will*</u>
<u>*recoup expense of deleting duplicate names on first mailing. We will enhance company image.*</u>

What's next? Who will do what, when, and how? <u>*I can begin the purge next Monday.*</u>

An E-mail without a Position—Revised

The following version is much more effective. For starters, the Position proposes action, which is prominently presented as the topic sentence of the second paragraph. Also, in the final sentence the writer indicates who is responsible for the next step. The opening paragraph indicates what triggered the memo—a request—and gets readers' attention by noting that the purge will pay for itself. The two Conclusions, prefaced with "First" and "Second," do a good job of substantiating the Position.

Finally, one of the Conclusions—that Calloway will recoup the expense of eliminating the duplicate names on their first mailing—is used in the opening paragraph to emphasize the importance of the recommended action.

> **Subject: Proposal to Purge 70,000 Duplicate Names in Promotion Database** ✔
>
> As you requested, I audited the promotional database and found there are approximately 70,000 duplicate names in the file [***What Prompts Your Document Now***]. My calculations indicate Calloway Computer will recoup the expense of eliminating these duplicate names on our first mailing [***Importance of Subject***].
>
> Therefore, I request your authorization to purge these duplicate names [***Position***] based on the following two considerations.
>
> First, the purge will pay for itself on the first mailing, as we will save $37,000 by eliminating the duplicate names. This $37,000 represents the extra costs of additional postage and of creating more mail pieces than required. Moreover, we will save this amount on each future mailing [***Conclusion***].
>
> Second, we will enhance our image among the 70,000 people who may question Calloway's business and computing savvy when they receive duplicate mailings [***Conclusion***].
>
> I am prepared to begin the purge next Monday after I see you at the staff meeting that morning [***Future Work***].

One-Paragraph E-Mails

The Printers E-mail

Another common practice when composing e-mail is putting the entire message in a single paragraph.

Effective e-mails are easy to scan and read selectively. Writing your message in a single paragraph defeats both objectives. Nothing stops a reader's eye faster than a large block of text, which must be read in its entirety to be understood. By breaking large paragraphs into their component topics, you enable readers to scan the information and focus on those topics that are most important to them.

Remember also that people often use their Inbox as a To-Do List. By presenting your information in short paragraphs and using bulleted or numbered lists, you make it easier for readers to give you the information you need or perform the task you have requested.

The following e-mail begins with a Position that appears straight-forward enough: "We will retire three of the four existing HP printers and purchase one new HP printer." The Position is followed, however, by a paragraph packed with decisions and requests, presented in no particular order, that the reader is supposed to act on. How easy will it be for the reader to know or remember what they are being asked to do? An outline of the contents of this paragraph follows.

Subject: Printers
Attachments: SGPrinters.xls

Fred,

I have an answer on the printers. We will retire three of the four existing HP printers and purchase one new HP printer. See if they will give us more credits for three printers. I need you to work with Gretchen and get all of the AS400 Queues that will have to be changed to the new printer. The new Printer will go near the FUJI Xerox and I will leave it up to you on which of the other three we replace. We will go with the metered option as listed in the attached spreadsheet. Depending on which cost is less per sheet for metered printing between the new HP and Fuji Xerox we will point the existing Windows print queues to that printer. Please raise a purchase request for this. Advise on time of delivery and coordinate the move of the queues. Thank you.

Regards,

Once again, the e-mail's main points have been summarized on the *Outline for E-mail and Texting* on the next page.

OUTLINE *for* E-MAIL *and* TEXTING

Subject: *HP Printer Purchase – Tasks to be Done*

What prompts your e-mail? *I have an answer about the printers*

What do you want your reader to do or believe? *We will retire 3 of 4 HP printers, purchase 1 new HP, and use the metered option listed in attached spreadsheet.*

Why? What are your reasons or points? *New HP will go near FUJI Xerox. Point Windows print queues to new HP or FUJI depending on cost per sheet for metered printing.*

What's next? Who will do what, when, and how? *Decide which HPs to retire. See if HP will give credit for retired printers. Request PO for new HP. Let me know when HP will arrive. Work with Gretchen to move AS400 Queues to new printer.*

The Printers E-mail—Revised

Although filling out an *Outline for E-mail and Texting* like the one above is a good way to plan an e-mail before you write, too often we are thinking and writing at the same time. In that case, we need a way to review what we have written and make it more readable.

The simplest approach to revising one-paragraph e-mails is to begin by breaking them into a separate paragraph for each topic discussed, as follows:

> **Subject:** Printers
> **Attachments:** SGPrinters.xls
>
> Fred,
>
> I have an answer on the printers.
>
> We will retire three of the four existing HP printers and purchase one new HP printer.
>
> See if they will give us more credits for three printers.
>
> I need you to work with Gretchen and get all of the AS400 Queues that will have to be changed to the new printer.
>
> The new Printer will go near the FUJI Xerox and I will leave it up to you on which of the other three we replace.
>
> We will go with the metered option as listed in the attached spreadsheet.
>
> Depending on which cost is less per sheet for metered printing between the new HP and Fuji Xerox we will point the existing Windows print queues to that printer.
>
> Please raise a purchase request for this.
>
> Advise on time of delivery and coordinate the move of the queues.
>
> Thank you.
>
> Regards,

Already the e-mail is easier to read and understand. Now, reorganize the paragraphs, grouping similar topics and presenting the information in descending order of importance.

> **Subject:** Printers
> **Attachments:** SGPrinters.xls
>
> Fred,
>
> I have an answer on the printers.
>
> We will retire three of the four existing HP printers and purchase one new HP printer.
>
> We will go with the metered option as listed in the attached spreadsheet.
>
> Depending on which cost is less per sheet for metered printing between the new HP and Fuji Xerox we will point the existing Windows print queues to that printer.
>
> The new Printer will go near the FUJI Xerox and I will leave it up to you on which of the other three we replace.
>
> See if they will give us more credits for three printers.
>
> Please raise a purchase request for this.
>
> Advise on time of delivery and coordinate the move of the queues.
>
> I need you to work with Gretchen and get all of the AS400 Queues that will have to be changed to the new printer.
>
> Thank you.
>
> Regards,

Now that we have established a logical order in which to present our information, we finalize the paragraphing, use a list to highlight key points, and write a more effective Subject line that identifies what we want the reader to do.

Notice in the rewrite on the next page how much detail appears when we break it out into separate paragraphs. Who knew that the original e-mail contained so much information and so many action items?

Subject: HP Printer Purchase—Tasks to be Done
Attachments: SGPrinters.xls

Fred,

I have an answer about the printers [***What Prompts Your Document Now***].

We will retire three of the four existing HP printers, purchase one new HP printer, and use the metered option listed in the attached spreadsheet [***Position***].

The new HP printer will go near the existing FUJI Xerox. We will point the existing Windows print queues either to the new HP or the FUJI Xerox, depending on which costs less per sheet for metered printing [***Conclusions***].

Please handle the following items related to the purchase [***Action Program***]:

- Decide which three of the other HP printers we should retire.
- See if HP will give us more credits for three printers.
- Request a purchase order for the new HP.
- Let me know when we can expect delivery.
- Work with Gretchen on moving all of the AS400 Queues that will have to be changed to the new printer.

Thank you.

Regards,

A Status Report E-mail

The following e-mail is a status report for a pipe inspection job. The e-mail packs so much detail into a single paragraph that the reader could miss the fact that there are two issues that need attention.

Shelby,

Pipe Professionals inspected 5811 ft of pipe last week and have inspected 14,937 ft thus far. In the past three weeks of inspections they have been averaging 5,000ft per week. No major operational or structural defects were encountered this week and the interceptors appear to be in relatively good shape. As we discussed last week the truck is out of town on another job this week and will resume inspections on Monday, September 18. Upon resumption of work, no further planned delays are scheduled for the remainder of the job. I estimate that Pipe Professionals is approximately 60% complete on their budget. If they proceed at their current rate, the budget should run out around 21,000 feet. Also, may I request that we update the LENS spreadsheet to reflect my billing rate as an Engineer II. I like to keep an eye on things to ensure that I'm not getting into trouble ☺

Thanks,

Jack

A Status Report E-mail—Revised

Rather than using the *Outline for E-mail and Texting*, let's revise the e-mail using the approach illustrated in the previous example. Begin by breaking the message into a separate paragraph for each topic:

Shelby,

Pipe Professionals inspected 5811 ft of pipe last week and have inspected 14,937 ft thus far. In the past three weeks of inspections they have been averaging 5,000ft per week.

No major operational or structural defects were encountered this week and the interceptors appear to be in relatively good shape.

As we discussed last week the truck is out of town on another job this week and will resume inspections on Monday, September 18. Upon resumption of work, no further planned delays are scheduled for the remainder of the job.

I estimate that Pipe Professionals is approximately 60% complete on their budget. If they proceed at their current rate, the budget should run out around 21,000 feet.

Also, may I request that we update the LENS spreadsheet to reflect my billing rate as an Engineer II. I like to keep an eye on things to ensure that I'm not getting into trouble ☺

Thanks,

Jack

Having identified the principal topics that the e-mail discusses, now identify the Position—no operational or structural defects were encountered and the interceptors are in good shape—and the Issues that need to be brought to the reader's attention:

> Shelby,
>
> No major operational or structural defects were encountered this week and the interceptors appear to be in relatively good shape.
>
> I estimate that Pipe Professionals is approximately 60% complete on their budget. If they proceed at their current rate, the budget should run out around 21,000 feet.
>
> Pipe Professionals inspected 5811 ft of pipe last week and have inspected 14,937 ft thus far. In the past three weeks of inspections they have been averaging 5,000ft per week.
>
> Also, may I request that we update the LENS spreadsheet to reflect my billing rate as an Engineer II. I like to keep an eye on things to ensure that I'm not getting into trouble ☺
>
> As we discussed last week the truck is out of town on another job this week and will resume inspections on Monday, September 18. Upon resumption of work, no further planned delays are scheduled for the remainder of the job.
>
> Thanks,
>
> Jack

The final rewrite uses this new ordering of the information, plus a bulleted list, to draw the reader's attention to the issues that need to be addressed.

> Shelby,　　　　　　　　　　　　　　　　　　　　　☑
>
> On the Pipe Professionals inspection project [***What Prompts Your Document Now***], no major operational or structural defects were encountered last week and the interceptors appear to be in relatively good shape [***Position***].
>
> There are, however, two issues you should be aware of [***Issues***]:
>
> - Pipe Professionals' budget may run out as early as week after next [***Conclusion***]. Pipe Professionals has already spent approximately 60% of their budget. If they proceed at their current rate, the budget should run out at around 21,000 feet.
>
>   In the past three weeks, they have been averaging 5,000 ft. per week. Pipe Professionals have inspected 14,937 ft. thus far, and they inspected 5811 ft of pipe last week [***Data***].
>
> - I think the LENS spreadsheet should reflect my billing rate as an Engineer II [***Conclusion***].
>
>   May I request that we update the spreadsheet accordingly [***Future Work***]? I like to keep an eye on things to ensure that I'm not getting into trouble ☺
>
> Also, as we discussed last week, the truck will be out of town on another job this coming week and will resume inspections on Monday, September 18. When work resumes, no further planned delays are scheduled for the remainder of the job [***Conclusion***].
>
> Thanks,
>
> Jack

Thinking As You Write

The Daily Forecast E-mail

Another common practice when writing e-mails is to present information in the order in which we did our thinking.

The result of composing and thinking at the same time is that key information is often buried at the end of the e-mail. To make sure readers don't miss this information, people frequently resort to CAPITALIZATION, **boldface** type, and <u>underlining</u> to try to get their readers' attention, as in the e-mail below.

Subject: Daily Forecasts for Q207

I know it's hard to believe but, it's that time again...

Dan has asked that I gather daily updates from everyone regarding a forecast of the bookings for the quarter. Please e-mail the attached form to me at the end of your day prior to leaving <u>starting Friday March 23rd</u>. Also, please remember that this is our estimate of what will book, not necessarily what is in the forecast. We have been very accurate in the past and Dan is counting on our input.

The daily updates should include:

Your forecast of <u>bookings for that day through the end of the quarter</u>. For example Friday 3/23, I should receive your forecast of bookings for 3/23 through 3/31. This would be your estimate of bookings for the remainder of the quarter and this <u>should</u> include any orders that were added to projections prior to leaving for the day as well as those that booked that day. THIS NUMBER SHOULD ALSO INCLUDE ORDERS CURRENTLY IN YOUR HOPPER NUMBER THAT YOU EXPECT TO BOOK.

The total in your Hopper (orders in the office that cannot be booked yet) <u>should not</u> include any orders that had been added to projections prior to leaving for the day.

Each of these numbers **should NOT** include any **Ultrasound** even though you might be processing at the regional level. I will get those numbers from Ultrasound.

The first day you should send to me is Friday 3/23 before you leave.

If anyone has any questions, just let me know.

Good luck to everyone with Quarter Close!!

The Daily Forecast E-mail—Revised

If you find yourself capitalizing words or bolding text in an e-mail to get readers' attention, consider putting the important information at the beginning of your e-mail instead.

In the rewrite below, you will notice that, rather than using capitalization and bolding, the structure of the e-mail is used to guide the readers' attention to the key information.

By presenting the most important information at the beginning of an e-mail, you make sure your readers won't miss it. And if you tell readers at the beginning what your message is about and why it is important, they are more likely to read your e-mail through to the details.

Subject: New Procedures for Daily Q207 Forecasts

I know it's hard to believe but… it's time to compile quarterly projections again…

Dan has asked that I gather daily updates from everyone regarding a forecast of bookings for the quarter [***What Prompts Your Document Now***]—that is, your estimate of what will book, not necessarily what is in the forecast [***Definition of Terms***]. We have been very accurate in the past and Dan is counting on your input [***Importance of Subject***].

To fulfill Dan's request, starting Friday, March 23, please e-mail the attached form to me at the end of your day prior to leaving [***Position***].

The daily updates should include [***Issues***]:

- Any orders that booked that day.
- Your forecast of bookings through the end of the quarter. For example, Friday 3/23, I should receive your forecast of bookings for 3/23 through 3/31.
- Any orders that were added to projections prior to leaving for the day.
- Orders currently in your Hopper number—orders in the office that cannot be booked yet—that you expect to book, except for orders that had been added to projections prior to leaving for the day.

Daily updates should not include Ultrasound bookings, even though you might be processing at the regional level. I will get those numbers from Ultrasound [***Issues***].

If anyone has any questions, just let me know [***Action Program***].

Good luck to everyone with Quarter Close!!

A Follow-up to a Sales Call

The following e-mail was sent as a follow-up to a sales call. And although the e-mail includes all the product information the prospect should receive, it misses an opportunity to continue the sales process.

The message fails to highlight the benefits of Seaside Solutions' products in a way that the reader can easily grasp. And in that respect, it fails to make the case for why the reader should purchase Seaside products.

Subject: Seaside Solutions Follow up

Ralph,

It was great speaking with you yesterday. Here is my contact information for your files. As I mentioned yesterday, Seaside Solutions manufactures a full line of products that offer low maintenance and high performance in a marine environment. We have been manufacturing WaterGuard and WaterLoc vinyl sheet piling for over 20 years and are now a standard material for building seawalls. Recently, I have seen our sheets being used in civil applications such as retention and detention ponds, cut off walls, baffle walls, dike cores, and retaining walls. Our products are versatile and can be used in many different applications.

In addition to sheet piling, we have added Standard Dock and Marine to our product line. Standard Dock has been in the dock building business for over 30 years, fabricating aluminum floating and fixed dock systems. With that being said, we have the ability to offer everything to build out a marina.

I have attached several links to our website. If you have any questions, please call me.

Thank you for your time and consideration.

Seaside Solutions: www.seaside.com/

Sheet Piling Specifications: www.seaside.com/sheetpiling/specs

Standard Docks: www.seaside.com/docks

Marine Piling and Timber: www.seaside.com/timbers

A Follow-up to a Sales Call—Revised

In contrast with the original, the rewrite below steps the reader through a logical presentation of product information that guides their attention to reasons why they should purchase Seaside Solutions' products. In this way, what was a haphazard and merely informational communication becomes part of a more effective and professional sales process.

Subject: Seaside Solutions—Product Overview

Ralph,

It was great speaking with you yesterday about your need for marine construction products [*What Prompts Your Document Now*].

As we discussed, Seaside Solutions manufactures the finest low maintenance and high performance marine construction materials available. Our versatile product line can be used in many different applications and includes everything needed to build out a marina [*Position*].

In particular, I would like to draw your attention to the following product lines [*Issues*]:

Vinyl sheet piling—The WaterGuard and WaterLoc sheet piling products are now standard material for building seawalls. They are also used in civil applications such as retention and detention ponds, cut off walls, baffle walls, dike cores, and retaining walls. The WaterGuard and WaterLoc product lines have been part of our product line for over 20 years.

Floating and fixed aluminum dock systems—Our Standard Dock and Marine Piling and Timber product lines have provided complete range of materials for dock construction for over 30 years.

Below are links to our website and more information on these product lines.

If you have any questions, please call or e-mail me via the numbers and addresses provided below [*Action Program*].

Thank you for your time and consideration.

Seaside Solutions: www.seaside.com/

Sheet Piling Specifications: www.seaside.com/sheetpiling/specs

Standard Docks: www.seaside.com/docks

Marine Piling and Timber: www.seaside.com/timbers

E-mails That Tell Stories

The Conference Call Report

In the following example, not only is the writer thinking as he writes, he is also writing as if he is talking to us. The e-mail tells a "he said-she said" story about a conference call he participated in, instead of reporting highlights of the discussion. As a result, the first paragraph is too long for readers to scan and easily understand.

Because we usually formulate what we want to say as we write e-mail, it is tempting to write in a style that is like unstructured conversation. But don't confuse the effectiveness of a conversational style, that can make writing more readable, with a casual approach that can make messages feel unprofessional.

Although e-mail exchanges often feel like the back-and-forth of a conversation, they still have to be written, and people have to read them, both of which require thinking. Therefore, as you write, pay attention to how you organize your information on the screen.

> Al,
>
> Just a quick summary of yesterday's Draftwriter meeting . . . . I dialed in to yesterday's Draftwriter meeting (it was scheduled for an hour, but lasted about thirty minutes). No progress to speak of; they went over the "project plan" that Jerome had circulated. There were still outstanding questions regarding the responses they received from the field; for example, someone felt that they needed to go back to the field to get more clarification on what was meant by "interest payments". Someone else also expressed a concern that for instances where the use of Draftwriter was deemed to be "inappropriate" (i.e., not fraudulent uses, but uses that were either prohibited by policy, or an avenue other than Draftwriter should have been used), nevertheless those uses may have set a bad precedent that creates an exposure for National Insurance. An example would be where someone used Draftwriter to "expedite" some payment to or on behalf of a customer. Now, with Draftwriter going away (along with the ability to process "expedited" payments), customers who previously benefited from that "consideration" could react negatively if a similar situation arises in the future, and they are told they can no longer expect the "quick resolution" that was extended to them in the past.
>
> Next steps: Another meeting in two to four weeks, to check on progress of steps contained in the "project plan", and to see if additional alternatives have been firmed up to cover all current uses of Draftwriter.

The Conference Call Report—Revised

Notice in the rewrite below how the use of lists highlights what took place during the conference call, and makes the information easier to assimilate. By separating different topics into paragraphs, it is easier to read and understand the detail.

Al,

I dialed in to yesterday's Draftwriter meeting. Here is a quick summary [***What Prompts Your Document Now***].

No progress to speak of. They went over the "project plan" that Jerome had circulated. Another meeting will be scheduled in two to four weeks to [***Position***]:

1. Check on progress of the "project plan", and
2. See if alternatives have been found to cover all current uses of Draftwriter.

The following issues were discussed based on questions raised from the field [***Issues***]:

- Should they go back to the field to get clarification on what was meant by "interest payments"?

- In instances where using Draftwriter was considered "inappropriate," did those uses set a bad precedent, creating an exposure for National?

  For example, customers for whom Draftwriter had been used to "expedite" a payment might react negatively if a similar situation arose, and they were told that the "quick resolution" extended to them in the past was no longer available.

  "Inappropriate" here does not mean fraudulent, but either prohibited by policy, or where an avenue other than Draftwriter should have been used.

I'll keep you posted as the discussion continues [***Future Work***].

The Lost Transactions E-mail

Explaining a problem and what needs to be done about it is often a complex task. The author of the following e-mail adopts a common approach to this difficult task: they tell a story—they give a narrative of facts and events. A better approach to defining a problem is to present a structured analysis of the facts that explains where we are now, how we got here, and what needs to happen next.

The headings in the following e-mail—Primary observation, Secondary observation, Other observation, and The plan—are an attempt to give the material a logical structure. What this e-mail fails to make clear, however, is why anyone needs to read and understand all this detail in the first place.

As for the opening apology for the length of the communication, either the detail in the e-mail is necessary—in which case no apology is needed—or it is unnecessary—in which case the detail should be left out. Either way, the apology wastes readers' time and probably tries their patience.

A good test of the readability of any long communication is to ask whether the reader can scan it and grasp the gist of its message. Try that test on this one.

Subject: Retail Store level problem—lost transactions—an outline

Hello to all.

Please forgive the length of this communication in advance. I wanted to be sure to give you as complete a picture of our plans as is possible.

As you are all aware, over the past several months our mutual teams have been working on the issue of "lost transactions" at the store level. Below I will attempt to summarize what we think we know, what we are doing and what our efforts are to resolve this issue at the root cause level. Please, please do jump in and set us on the right path if you believe you have information that differs or that will assist us in solving this issue, permanently. The Information Technology team is most anxious to get to the bottom of this problem.

Primary observation: The problem with lost transactions, which manifests itself as a register "locking up" in most cases, seems to occur at heavier volume stores during high transaction traffic periods. Amanda has provided a list of the stores that experienced/reported problems to us over this past weekend.

Secondary observation: The problem seems to have appeared/increased frequency at/about the time that the new back office PC's were installed. It does not seem likely that the DSL installation is part of the issue, as the DSL network is NOT used for register to back office PC communication. Having said this, we do intend to investigate all corners of the technology implemented at the store level. DSL network will be a secondary consideration.

Other observation: We have not been successful in isolating the issue to date, thus we are going to go to the next level of troubleshooting, with committed and dedicated resources.

The plan: Technical team members with Retail Store knowledge are working diligently to try to isolate the cause of these failures. Please understand that we have in recent months changed all hardware, all software, the network infrastructure as well as changed a multitude of configurations. It does take time to try and determine what is truly wrong. We are in "critical mode" and have dedicated resources to the issue who will remain with the issue until there is valid progress in resolving. The team members have explicit instructions to escalate to their management team for help when/if this is required.

The team will pick approximately 6 stores from the list Amanda provided as a "work group" for our troubleshooting. These stores will be identified to all once chosen. (Today or early tomorrow)

A rigid methodology will be followed for any/all changes to these stores, and documented. Any change will be exactly applied to the "work group". Given the problem does seem to only present itself at certain "peak" time periods, changes will have to be in place for an extended period of time or until a problem is once again discovered in order to be deemed a success or not. (Depending on if further problems are experienced, success or failure of that particular change.)

Some of the items we need to investigate are software package incompatibility, (one by one) hardware configuration/incompatibility, network traffic between the register and back office PC's, PC processes that may be interfering with proper register communication.

The technical team has instructions to send out an update each day as to their activities, discoveries, changes, etc. I need to ask Amanda for her very valuable assistance, in ensuring that the technical team (and myself) are copied on any reports of lost transactions at the store level, as soon as she knows. (Any store)

Jesse Danforth will be responsible for the day to day oversight of this effort.

NOTE—SRS is a helpful partner. Their first level troubleshooting "concern" is getting the store back up and running as quickly as possible, as it should be. I ask everyone to please consider this as we move forward with this effort. Most of the time with this particular problem, rebooting the back office PC is the absolute correct answer to ensure continued operation. We will ask SRS to also report these types of "incidents" to us directly, even if the problem is "resolved" because the store is working again. We will rely on SRS in this effort from the "first level troubleshooting" perspective.

Regards,

The Lost Transactions E-mail—Revised

Since the purpose of the original e-mail was to ask people for input about the lost transactions problem, the following rewrite moves specific information about the problem to the beginning of the e-mail. Apologies and reassurances are either left out or moved to later in the e-mail. And once again, numbered and bulleted lists are used to help readers navigate the quantity of information included.

Subject: Your Input Needed to Resolve Retail Store Lost Transaction Problem

Hello to all.

As you are all aware, over the past several months our teams have been working on the "lost transactions" issue at the store level. Summarized below is what we think we know, what we are currently doing, and what we are going to do to get at the root cause of the issue. The communication is long because I want to give everyone as complete a picture of our plans as possible [*What Prompts Your Document Now*].

Since the Information Technology team is anxious to resolve this problem, please contact Jesse Danforth if you have information that differs from what I report here or that might help us to solve the issue. Jesse is responsible for day-to-day management of the effort [*Position*].

Amanda, please notify the technical team and me as soon as you receive any reports of lost transactions at any store. This will be very helpful [*Issue*].

What We Think We Know [*Issues*]:

1. The problem usually manifests as a register "locking up". It seems to occur at stores with heavier volume, and during periods of high transaction traffic.
2. The problem seems to have appeared or increased around the time the new back office PC's were installed.
3. Amanda has a list of stores that experienced or reported problems this past weekend.
4. The DSL installation does not seem to be part of the problem, since DSL is NOT used for register-to-back-office PC communication. Therefore, the DSL network will be a secondary consideration, although we intend to investigate all corners of the technology implemented at the store level.

Our Troubleshooting Plan [*Issues*]:

Technical team members with Retail Store knowledge are working to isolate the cause of the failures. Today or early tomorrow, the team will pick approximately 6 stores from the list Amanda provided as a "work group" for troubleshooting. When the stores have been chosen, everyone will be notified.

A rigid methodology will be followed and documented for all changes to these stores. All changes will be applied to all stores in the "work group". Since the problem only seems to occur during "peak" time periods, changes will be maintained for an extended period or until a problem is discovered, and we can tell whether or not the change is a success.

Components We Intend To Investigate [*Issues*]:

- Software package compatibility (one by one)
- Hardware configuration and compatibility
- Network traffic between the register and back office PC's
- PC processes that may be interfering with register communication.

Please understand that figuring out what is wrong is taking time because we have changed all hardware, all software, and the network infrastructure in recent months, as well as a multitude of configurations [*Essential Background*].

Because we haven't isolated the problem yet, we are in "critical mode" and have dedicated technical team members to the next level of troubleshooting. They will be working on the issue until it is substantially resolved. Team members have instructions to escalate to their management team for help when required. The technical team will also send daily updates about their activities, discoveries, changes, etc [*Essential Background*].

Also, relative to SRS, everyone please remember that we rely on SRS and that they are a helpful partner in this effort. We are asking SRS to report these "incidents" to us directly, even if the problem is "resolved" because the store is working again. As it should be, their first level troubleshooting "concern" is getting the store back up and running as quickly as possible [*Issue*].

Regards,

2. Five Muddled Mysteries:
Originals and Revisions

THIS CHAPTER CONTINUES TO ILLUSTRATE THE IMPORTANCE OF structure to the clarity of a document that we began in the last chapter. Whereas the last chapter looked at how to improve the effectiveness of e-mails, this chapter examines the importance of a well-structured argument in memos.

The distinction between an e-mail and a memo is difficult to make these days, given that memos are usually sent electronically. Some of the examples in the previous chapter on e-mail could be described as memos.

In simplest terms, however, the difference between an e-mail and a memo resides primarily in the tone or formality of the document. A memo is often used to establish the terms of an agreement, transaction, or contract, and in that respect carries the weight of a legal document. Therefore, people usually make a greater effort to structure the presentation of their information in a memo than in an e-mail. As the following examples reveal, however, they don't always succeed in doing so effectively.

Gamma Logging Revisited

In *Organizing Ideas* you have seen a clear Opening Statement for a memo on gamma logging. To emphasize how important the sequencing of information is, however, you will see on the next page the original Mystery Story on gamma logging from which the Opening Statement in *Organizing Ideas* was composed.

The first question is what's the Position? It's not up front, so it's probably at the end. And there it is, but stated rather equivocally: "From the geo-technical point of view. . . . gamma logging could possibly be. . ." and so forth.

So what is the writer really proposing? Yes, the writer believes gamma logging is cost-justified. But let's call for action—"I recommend we perform gamma logging."

Now read through the memo and pick out the Conclusions. I find four supporting this Position and one concern.

Once you have identified the positive and negative Conclusions, look for the other elements of the structure, such as the Essential Background and Definition of Terms. Also, consider what might be appropriate Recommendations stating the Action Program and Future Work. And what could you mention at the beginning that would get the readers' attention?

Finally, this memo is not just poorly organized, it is contradictory and confusing. In the third paragraph the writer says the personnel and equipment are available. But in the paragraph immediately after the table, the writer claims the $7,140 does not include the cost of personnel and equipment. So is the $4,000 in addition to the $7,140? Only the writer knows.

Subject: Gamma Logging in the Natuna Boreholes

I have contacted the consulting firms of Armstrong & Dodds, Lester Young Associates, and the Rushing Group and discussed the possibility of performing gamma logging in the Natuna boreholes. This memo reports the results of the discussions with these consultants.

Stratigraphy is a branch of geology that uses various techniques to determine the composition of subsurface rock formations. Petroleum geologists use this data to predict where oil reservoirs may exist, and how difficult drilling to the reservoir will be.

Gamma logging is one of the primary methods used for determining soil stratigraphy. By measuring the naturally occurring gamma radiation in a borehole, geologists can map the porosity of rock or sediment around a well hole. By way of background, the Natuna boreholes are located 400 miles off the coast of Malaysia, where we have been conducting explorations for the past 18 months.

Gamma logging can be collected in the drill pipe. Usually, logging in the drill pipe is an easy and fast operation. It takes approximately two hours to log one 500-foot borehole. All three of these consultants indicate that they have experienced personnel to do both the logging and soil sampling. Thus, no additional personnel are required to be sent on board the investigating vessel. Both Armstrong & Dodds and the Rushing Group have their own drill pipe. Lester Young Associates rents the equipment from subcontractors.

The vessel motion, which is the up and down movement of the vessel, creates problems in interpreting the logging record. If the vessel motion is great, the data may not be reliable. Armstrong & Dodds recommends that the maximum tolerable vessel motion is 1.5 feet. A motion compensator may be required equipment on the vessel in order to minimize the vessel motion to a tolerable level. The necessity of the motion compensator depends on the type of vessel that will be used.

The estimate of the additional cost of performing gamma logging in the Natuna boreholes is below $10,000 dollars. Based on the information given by Armstrong & Dodds, the breakdown of the cost is listed as follows.

Item	Cost
Logging equipment, estimated 14 days total at $110/day	$1,540
Logging footage charges, 3 boreholes at approx. $1,200/hole	3,600
Mob and demob of 300 lb. logging equipment	2,000
Total	$7,140

Comments

The gamma logging data provides a continuous qualitative record of soil stratigraphy over the entire depth of the borehole. It allows one to define more accurately the boundaries and the gradational changes of the strata. From the geotechnical point of view, the value of the information to be obtained from gamma logging could possibly be well worth the extra cost.

WORKSHEET FOR ORGANIZING IDEAS—Short Form

SUBJECT: *Gamma Logging in the Natuna Boreholes - Recommended*

OPENING STATEMENT—*What information do you need to include?*

1 **I. Significance to the Readers**

    A. What Prompts Your Document Now? *Contacted Armstrong & Dodds, Lester Young Associates, and the Rushing Group to discuss gamma logging*

    B. Importance of Subject: *They think gamma logging will give more extensive record of soil stratigraphy*

2 **II. Position:** *Recommend performing gamma logging at the Natuna site*

7   **A. Essential Background:** *Natuna boreholes located 400 miles off Malaysia where we have been exploring for past 18 months*

8   **B. Definition of Terms:** *Stratigraphy studies subsurface rock formations; Gamma logging determines porosity of rock or sediment*

    III. Methodology (if necessary)

    __   **A. Sources of Data:** _____

    __   **B. Assumptions & Limitations:** _____

    IV. Issues and Conclusions

3 **PRO**	**4** **CON**
1. *Provides soil stratigraphy*	1. *Unreliable data/vessel motion*
2. *Reasonable cost*	2. _____
3. *Easy to perform*	3. _____
4. *Have personnel & equipment*	4. _____
5. _____	5. _____

    V. Recommendations

5   **A. Action Program:** *Get back to me with decision by end of the week*

6   **B. Future Work:** *Then can begin to get the equipment ready if you decide to go ahead*

↑   *What is the best order in which to present your information?*

Gamma Logging Revisited—Revised

The following revision, which was composed from the previous *Worksheet*, is a great improvement over the original version. Although readers may not be familiar with gamma logging, the logical structure of the revision will make it clear what the writer is proposing and the reasons.

Formatting the memo as a one-page Opening Statement, with the Data presented in an attachment, makes it much easier to sort through the details.

The subject line now conveys the Position and the opening paragraph does an effective job of getting the memo started. Also, the Position is prominently presented as the topic sentence of the second paragraph.

In the listing of Conclusions, the matters of "no additional personnel" and "availability of equipment" are combined into one Conclusion because they are related points and there was limited Data for each.

In terms of the order of the Conclusions, a little reflection reveals that there is a logic to their presentation. If "the record of soil stratigraphy" isn't needed, then "cost" and "easy and fast operation" are incidental considerations. So, the need for the soil record should be established first, before the additional benefits of gamma logging can be argued.

Relative to "vessel motion," if the problem is acknowledged in the Opening Statement, as it should be, then the solution using a motion compensator needs to be included as well. Otherwise the reader would have to turn to the *Vessel Motion* sideheading in the attachment to see if the problem can be resolved. The matter is put to rest in the Opening Statement by adding the line "However, this problem can be corrected with a motion compensator."

Finally, if it is any help in reading the list of costs in the table, "mob" and "demob" are jargon for "mobilize" and demobilize.

Subject: Gamma Logging in the Natuna Boreholes—Recommended

I have spoken with engineers at three consulting firms—Armstrong & Dodds, Lester Young Associates, and the Rushing Group—and discussed the possibility of performing gamma logging in the Natuna boreholes [*What Prompts Your Document Now*]. They all agree that gamma logging will give us a much more extensive record of soil stratigraphy with which to identify the characteristics of the strata [*Importance of Subject*].

Therefore, I recommend we perform gamma logging at the Natuna site [*Position*].

Based on my conversations, there are four reasons for conducting the logging:

1. Gamma logging will meet our need for a record of soil stratigraphy
2. The cost is reasonable
3. The logging is easy to perform
4. The personnel and equipment are available to do the logging [*Conclusions*].

My only reservation is that vessel motion could cause the data to be unreliable. However, this problem can be corrected with a motion compensator [*Conclusion*].

Each of these considerations is addressed in the attachment.

I would appreciate your getting back to me with your decision by the end of the week [*Action Program*]. Then I can begin to get the equipment ready if you decide to go ahead with the gamma logging [*Future Work*].

By way of background, the Natuna boreholes are located 400 miles off the coast of Malaysia. We have been conducting explorations there for the past 18 months [*Essential Background*].

Stratigraphy is a branch of geology that uses various techniques to determine the composition of subsurface rock formations. Petroleum geologists use this data to predict where oil reservoirs may exist, and how difficult drilling to the reservoir will be.

Gamma logging is one of the primary methods used for determining soil stratigraphy. By measuring the naturally occurring gamma radiation in a borehole, geologists can map the porosity of rock or sediment around a well hole. [*Definition of Terms*].

Attachment

Attachment—Gamma Logging in the Natuna Boreholes

1. Need for Record

To ensure accurate evaluation of the Natuna boreholes, we need to have a continuous qualitative record of soil stratigraphy over the entire depth of the borehole. Gamma logging data will provide this information, enabling us to define the boundaries and the gradational changes of the strata more accurately [*Data*].

2. Reasonable Cost

The estimated cost of performing gamma logging in the Natuna boreholes is a little over $11,000, including charges for the vessel, equipment, and personnel. Armstrong & Dodds estimated the cost of the logging equipment and services at $7,140 while the Rushing Group said the total cost of the vessel equipment and personnel would be about $4,000 [*Data*]. Therefore, total projected costs are as follows:

Table—Costs for Gamma Logging

Item	Cost
Logging equipment, estimated 14 days total at $110/day	$1,540
Logging footage charges, 3 boreholes at approx. $1,200/hole	3,600
Mob and demob of 300 lb. logging equipment	2,000
Subtotal	7,140
Vessel, related equipment, and personnel	4,000
Total	$11,140

3. Easy and Fast Operation

Gamma logging can be collected in the drill pipe. Usually, logging in the drill pipe is an easy and fast operation. It takes approximately two hours to log one 500-foot borehole [*Data*].

4. Availability of Personnel and Equipment

All three of the consultants I spoke with said they currently have experienced personnel and equipment available to do both the logging and soil sampling. Thus, no additional personnel are needed on board the vessel. Armstrong & Dodds and the Rushing Group have their own drill pipe, while Lester Young Associates rents that equipment from subcontractors [*Data*].

5. Correction for Vessel Motion

Vessel motion, or the up and down movement of a ship, can create problems in the interpretation and reliability of the logging record. Armstrong & Dodds recommends that vessel motion be kept to a maximum of 1.5 feet, which may require the use of a motion compensator. The necessity for the motion compensator will depend on the type of vessel used and on ocean conditions during the logging [*Data*].

A Memo Weighing Alternatives

One of the most common tasks in business is to evaluate alternatives and recommend the best course of action. In reporting on such an evaluation, people frequently think they have to discuss all the alternatives they considered as part of the justification for the action they recommend. Not necessarily so, as the following example illustrates.

The following memo examines five alternatives for providing accounting services to a manufacturing plant. At first, the structure appears sound, especially since we see the options listed in the Opening Statement and then addressed in the same order in the Body.

But where's the Position? It is not until the end of the two-and-a-half-page account that we find out the preferred course of action. The writer's approach appears to be a process of elimination. But why is the discussion of the preferred option buried in the middle of the four others?

Fortunately, we have all the pieces of this puzzle. We need only place them in the appropriate spaces on a *Worksheet* and then compose our revised account.

Subject: Visit to Hampton Enterprises

My visit to Hampton Enterprises was for the purpose of evaluating the feasibility and desirability of moving their accounting functions to Houston. I spent two days talking to Charles Christian about the current accounting systems and computer at Hampton and what might make sense for them in the future.

There have been minor changes in the accounting systems in the 14 months since I last visited. These changes relate primarily to approvals and schedules required by the Foods Division. The bulk of the accounting functions continue to be slow and unreliable, reflecting the outdated nature of the server they have. In fact, it was not working most of the time I was there, either because of the hardware or because of the software.

Charles was fully aware of the purpose of my visit and was most helpful. He and I discussed the five options which I saw for Hampton:

1. Keep the status quo;
2. Keep accounting operations in Memphis, but use an outside service bureau;
3. Keep accounting operations in Memphis, but purchase a new server;
4. Keep accounting operations in Memphis, using the Houston mainframe via network;
5. Move accounting operations to Houston.

I believe keeping the current system is not an option. While I was there, the server was down the entire first day, so that no processing could be done. Among other things, this meant that no order entry could be done and that bills of lading had to be done by hand in several instances. The second day the server was running but made some errors in part of the payroll run.

The second option, using an outside service bureau, is more attractive. It takes the computer operations and problems out of their hands. Since they have no computer experts on site, it would remove a major source of aggravation. It does have the drawback of having to batch items and get them to and from the service bureau. Turnaround time and possible customization of reports are two questions which would have to be addressed before deciding to go with this option and before choosing a service bureau.

A new server, the third option, has several advantages. Computer technology has advanced substantially over the past five years so that their current server, which cost $10,000 five years ago, could be replaced with something far more powerful for far less money—perhaps $5,000. There are numerous financial packages which would meet their needs, are relatively easy to use, and are fairly inexpensive. This option would give them control rather than having it outside. It does have the disadvantages of needing outside service should something go wrong and of still having the same staff who are averse to change.

The fourth option, networking Memphis into the Houston mainframe, allows control to remain in Memphis. It also makes use of an existing resource in Houston and would allow Hampton's staff to get help from Corporate Information Services. It would require four networked computers, although this hardware is relatively inexpensive. Other costs will include establishing and configuring the network, as well as establishing and maintaining the network's security. This option will also require working with the same staff which does not like change. Finally, there is a question of the flexibility of our current systems to allow integration of our accounting systems with theirs.

The final option is to move all the accounting functions to Houston. This is attractive for a couple of reasons: it makes use of the existing hardware in Houston, and the staff could be reduced in Memphis. However, Hampton would continue to require some hardware and some staff there, at least for printing bills of lading. Based on our goal numbers, we would need another person in both Accounts Payable and Payroll, and two additional persons in Billing to handle the extra volume. There is again the question of integration of Hampton into the Foods Division ledgers and chart of accounts. Hampton's is a less complex business, and we would have to combine it into an extremely complex accounting system. Finally, if we decide to sell Hampton, it would no longer be an autonomous unit, and it might be more difficult to separate it from the other Division entities.

Based on my analysis, I believe the most desirable option is to buy a new server and software for Hampton after devoting sufficient time and study to determine their specific needs.

I will be happy to discuss this with you further at your convenience.

Regards,

WORKSHEET FOR ORGANIZING IDEAS—*Short Form*

SUBJECT: _Moving Hampton Accounting to Houston—Not Recommended_

OPENING STATEMENT—*What information do you need to include?*

__1__ I. Significance to the Readers

    A. What Prompts Your Document Now? _March 12 and 13 visit to Hampton_ _Enterprises to evaluate moving accounting functions to Houston_

    B. Importance of Subject: _Accounting systems slow and unreliable, especially for_ _approvals and schedules_

__2__ II. Position: _Hampton's accounting functions should not be moved to Houston_

    __ A. Essential Background: _____

    __ B. Definition of Terms: _____

    III. Methodology (if necessary)

__6__   A. Sources of Data: _Two days talking with Christian / considered keeping status quo,_ _using service bureau, and networking with Houston computer_

    __ B. Assumptions & Limitations: _____

    IV. Issues and Conclusions

__4__ PRO	__3__ CON
1. _Need for Hampton staff/hardware_	1. _Use of Houston hardware_
2. _Difficulty of integrating systems_	2. _Reduction of Memphis staff_
3. _Problems separating systems_	3.
4.	4.
5.	5.

    V. Recommendations

__5__ A. Action Program: _Propose Hampton purchase more powerful server and related_ _software—cheaper, better software, more control over Hampton problems—need_ _for outside service of problems, resistance to change_

__7__ B. Future Work: _Look forward to discussing this with you_

    ↑ *What is the best order in which to present your information?*

A Memo Weighing Alternatives—Revised

The change that makes this memo readily understandable is the presentation of the Position as the topic sentence of the second paragraph. Once the Position is clear, the rest of the document can be structured to provide the necessary support.

Note also that the discussion of the unacceptable alternatives is left to an attachment as optional information. Consequently, readers who are convinced by the Conclusions for the Position do not need to turn to the attachment for any additional substantiation. By the same token, those who want to see the details can find the Data they need in the attachment.

Subject: Moving Hampton Accounting to Houston—Not Recommended ☑

On March 12 and 13, I visited Hampton Enterprises to evaluate moving their accounting functions to Houston [*What Prompts Your Document Now*]. Because their server is outdated, most of the accounting systems are slow and unreliable. This situation persists despite changes to the accounting system in the 14 months since I last visited, primarily in approvals and schedules required by the Foods Division [*Importance of Subject*].

Based on my assessment, I recommend that Hampton's accounting functions not be moved to Houston [*Position*]. While the move would make use of hardware in Houston and the Memphis staff could be reduced [*Conclusions*], there are three disadvantages.

- Hampton would still require accounting staff and hardware.
- Integrating Hampton's simple accounting system into the Food Division's complex system would be difficult.
- If Hampton were sold, it would be difficult to remove Hampton from Houston's accounting system [*Conclusions*].

As an alternative, I propose that Hampton purchase a more powerful server and related software [*Action Program*]. This option is attractive because:

1. Hampton could purchase a far more powerful server for as little as $5,000
2. Numerous financial packages exist that are more integrated, easier to use, and less expensive than their present software
3. Hampton would have greater control than if they relied on Houston [*summary of justification for Action Program*].

Two possible disadvantages are that Hampton would requirement outside service should something go wrong with the new server, and Hampton staff is resistant to change [*disadvantages of Action Program*]. These drawbacks will diminish as time passes, however, and are outweighed by the advantages noted above [*Conclusion*].

In evaluating the Hampton situation, I also considered three other solutions, based on two days discussing Hampton's accounting needs with Charles Christian. None of the alternatives, however, was satisfactory, for reasons discussed in the attachment [*Conclusion*]. I considered:

A. Maintaining the status quo
B. Using a service bureau in Memphis
C. Networking with the Houston mainframe [*Sources of Data*].

I look forward to discussing my proposed solution with you further [***Future Work***].

Regards,

Attachment

Attachment—Rejected Alternatives for Hampton Accounting

A.   Maintaining the Status Quo

Keeping the current system is not a valid option [***Conclusion***]. During my visit, no processing could be done because the server was down the entire first day. This meant that no order entry could be done and bills of lading had to be prepared by hand in several instances. The second day, the server was running but made errors in the payroll run [***Data***].

B.   Using an Outside Service Bureau

Using an outside service bureau is not a satisfactory solution either because it does not take computer operations and problems out of Hampton's hands [***Conclusion***]. Since they have no computer experts on site, it would remove a major source of aggravation.

Having to batch items and get them to and from the service bureau is, however, a major drawback. Turnaround time and possible customization of reports are also questions that would have to be addressed before going with this option or choosing a service bureau [***Data***].

C.   Networking with the Houston Mainframe

Although networking Memphis into the Houston mainframe would keep control of accounting in Memphis, it would also create more problems than it would solve [***Conclusion***].

The advantages of this option are that it makes use of a resource in Houston and would allow Hampton's staff to get help from Corporate Information Services.

On the other hand, four networked computers would be needed. Although this hardware is relatively inexpensive, other costs will include establishing and configuring the network, as well as establishing and maintaining network security. This option would also require working with the same staff that does not like change. Finally, it is questionable whether our accounting system is flexible enough to be integrated with Houston's system [***Data***].

An Informational Memo, When Action Would Be Better

The following memo is the cover page to a table of information about property easements that is attached to it. The memo is written as a merely informational communication, as if no action were required. A closer reading suggests, however, that by assuming an apparently disinterested, purely informational style, the writer is missing an opportunity to advocate action and advance the project.

The apparent purpose of the memo is to send the easement information to the Department of Environmental Services (DES) with the hope that DES will begin talking with property owners and tenants soon, and thereby avoid delays in the design and construction phases of the project. But the memo is too diplomatic. Instead of saying, "Here's the information, and here's what we need to do with it," it merely says, "Here's the information." How likely is the Project Manager at DES to act on a request for action that is not explicitly stated?

Even if the memo's purpose were merely informational, what easements does the project need? It is difficult to know without reading every single word.

TO: City of Habersham, Department of Environmental Services
FROM: Smith and Higgins Environmental Services
PROJECT NO.: DES Project 7503; Smith and Higgins Project 135426-09.15
SUBJECT: Property/Easement Requirements—Segment 1

Introduction

As the Dartmouth Force Main project approaches the 30% level of design, specific assumptions have been made with regard to property and easement requirements. These assumptions include temporary construction easements and permanent easements for the force main, air/vacuum valve vaults and access manholes facilities. There are also temporary easements for vehicle access to the construction sites and permanent access requirements that will be required to maintain the finished facilities. In addition, there are property needs for construction staging and storage of materials.

The purpose of this memorandum is to provide an early identification of the property/easement requirements that are anticipated at this time along the alignment of the Dartmouth Force Main. These anticipated property requirements are summarized in the attached Table 1. While these property requirements are not presented in a detailed manner, they are listed and described in a manner that can start discussions between DES and the impacted property owners and tenants.

The owner/tenant should be made aware of the project as it relates to their property, the anticipated requirements for each property and how the property may be affected. These requirements and needs should be communicated with the owner/tenant to obtain comments from them that will minimize impacts to their operations. When the design is complete and the easements have been finalized, it will then be possible to obtain contractor compliance with the already defined construction conditions, and, after construction has been completed, to satisfy DES requirements for the maintenance and repair of the force main.

WORKSHEET FOR ORGANIZING IDEAS—Short Form

SUBJECT: <u>Property Easement Requirements for Dartmouth Force Main Project</u>

OPENING STATEMENT—*What information do you need to include?*

1 **I. Significance to the Readers**

    A. What Prompts Your Document Now? <u>Need to identify easements required</u> <u>during construction and after project completion</u>

    B. Importance of Subject: <u>Easements need to be finalized before design is finalized</u> <u>to ensure contractors' compliance</u>

2 **II. Position:** <u>DES needs to begin communicating with owners and tenants now to get</u> <u>comments and minimize impact</u>

3 **A. Essential Background:** <u>Although easement list is not detailed, it is sufficient to</u> <u>start discussions</u>

___ **B. Definition of Terms:** _____

    III. Methodology (if necessary)

    A. Sources of Data: _____

___ **B. Assumptions & Limitations:** _____

    IV. Issues and Conclusions

    Project requires permanent and temporary easements for:

4 ~~PRO~~	___ ~~CON~~
1. <u>1. Force main</u>	**1.** <u>3. Vehicle access to construction sites</u>
2. <u>Air/vacuum valve vaults</u>	**2.** <u>4. Permanent access for facility maintenance</u>
3. <u>Access manholes</u>	**3.** _____
4. <u>2. Construction staging</u>	**4.** _____
5. <u>Materials storage</u>	**5.** _____

    V. Recommendations

___ **A. Action Program:** _____

___ **B. Future Work:** _____

What is the best order in which to present your information?

An Informational Memo, When Action Would Be Better—Revised

The rewrite below makes explicit information and objectives that were present, but obscured in the original memo. Rather than burying the easement requirements for the project in dense informational writing that takes no Position, the rewrite makes a clear, but diplomatic call for DES to act on the easement information now, and outlines what easements are needed.

Although issues can be presented in a strictly informational manner, see below how the consideration about the easements takes on a new character when it is presented as the basis for decision making and action. The more action-oriented rewrite is almost engaging in comparison with the original, which is not likely to get readers' attention.

TO: City of Habersham, Department of Environmental Services
FROM: Smith and Higgins Environmental Services
PROJECT NO.:   DES Project 7503; Smith and Higgins Project 135426-09.15
SUBJECT: Property Easement Requirements for Dartmouth Force Main
                        Project—Segment 1

Introduction

As the design for the Dartmouth Force Main project approaches 30% completion, it is important that we identify the property easements that the project will require during both construction and after the project is finished [***What Prompts Your Document Now***]. The anticipated property requirements are summarized in the attached Table 1.

These easements need to be finalized before the design is compete to ensure that contractors comply with these property conditions. After construction is complete, furthermore, DES will need these easements to maintain and repair the force main [***Importance of Subject***].

Therefore, DES needs to begin soon to communicate to property owners and tenants how the project will affect each property, and the easements that will be needed. That way, we can get owners' and tenants' comments and minimize the impacts to their operations [***Position***].

Although the attached table does not present the property requirements in detail, the list and descriptions are sufficient for DES to start discussions with the affected property owners and tenants [***Essential Background***].

In particular, the project will require both temporary construction easements and permanent easements for the following situations [***Issues***]:

- The force main, air/vacuum valve vaults, and access manholes facilities
- Construction staging and storage of materials
- Vehicle access to the construction sites
- Permanent access to maintain the finished facilities

Medical Benefits Memo

The following memo about next year's benefit package is trying to accomplish a number of purposes. The writer primarily wants all employees to submit their insurance enrollment forms in the next two weeks. But if they are going to do so, employees also need to know what they are signing up for, and an explanation for the change in insurance carriers.

As formulated in the original version on the next page, these purposes get jumbled into one informational communication. To compensate for the memo's complex organization, the writer tries to get readers' attention at the bottom of the second page with a liberal use of capitalized headings and bold and italicized text. But to what avail? Can we really be sure that everyone is going to read that far? If they do, it will only be because the welfare and that of their families is at stake. There has to be a better way to give people the information they need.

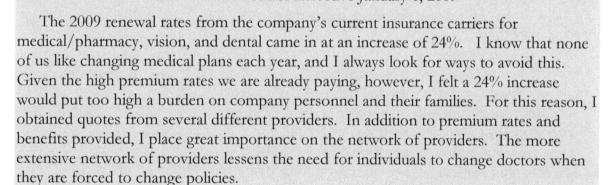

TO:	All Employees
FROM:	Office Manager
DATE:	December 5, 2008
RE:	Medical Benefit Policies Effective January 1, 2009

The 2009 renewal rates from the company's current insurance carriers for medical/pharmacy, vision, and dental came in at an increase of 24%. I know that none of us like changing medical plans each year, and I always look for ways to avoid this. Given the high premium rates we are already paying, however, I felt a 24% increase would put too high a burden on company personnel and their families. For this reason, I obtained quotes from several different providers. In addition to premium rates and benefits provided, I place great importance on the network of providers. The more extensive network of providers lessens the need for individuals to change doctors when they are forced to change policies.

Premiums

Although I could not find a medical benefits package with rates comparable to those we currently pay, I was able to put together a package with rate increases averaging 9%. To lessen the financial impact on families, the Cafeteria contributions for 2009 will increase for each employee from $425 to $490 per month (an increase of 15.3%).

Benefits

The attached Comparison of Medical Benefits spreadsheet outlines a comparison of our current plan benefits with those offered in 2009. Although some items are difficult to compare straight across the board, I believe the policies offered in 2009 represent an increase in benefits.

Provider Network

The network of providers is very extensive, and I hope no one is faced with the need to change doctors. In the enclosed packet, you will find Provider Directories for Vision and Alternative Care services. The much larger directory for physicians can be accessed at my desk. You can also go online at www.healthplan.com for a complete listing. If you find that you must change providers, please let me know. There are procedures you and your physician can take to get your physician included in the network. I can help you with that.

Summary Materials Enclosed

Comparison of Medical Benefits (current Plan with 2009 Plan) – *YELLOW SHEET*

- Employee Benefit Overview
- Group Number will be provided once all enrollment forms are submitted and processed. If we can get all enrollment forms submitted to the carrier by December 18, there is a good chance that everyone will receive their membership cards by January 1.
- Who Do I Call for Help?
- The PMK Group is our new Broker/Customer Service representative. They are the exclusive representatives for the Medical/Vision Plan we obtained through the Idaho Small Business Alliance Group. To consolidate and give us only one point of contact, they are also servicing our Dental, Life, STD, and LTD Plans. You can contact them directly whenever you have concerns or questions regarding any of the policies.

Enrollment Forms (Stapled Together) For Completion After All Materials Are Reviewed (Due to Office by End of Day December 17, 2008)

Benefit Election & Payroll Deduction Authorization form – BLUE SHEET

- Health Plan Enrollment Form (Medical/Pharmacy/Vision Benefits)
  - On the top section, check the following boxes:
    - PPO
    - Open Enrollment
  - If you are declining, just complete the "Employee Information" and "I Decline" sections, and sign/date the form.
- Universal Health Care Enrollment Form (Dental)
  - To enroll, complete Sections A, B, C, D, F
  - To waive coverage, complete Sections A, E, F
- Adelphi Financial Group—Life Insurance Beneficiary Designation Form
  - All employees are automatically covered and need to complete this form.

Supplemental Materials

Health Plan Packet—Medical/Pharmacy/Vision Benefits

Universal Health Care Packet—Dental Coverage Outlined

Adelphi Financial Group

    Summary of Life and AD&D Insurance

    Summary of Short-Term Disability Insurance

    Summary of Long-Term Disability Insurance

DUE DATE

We need to have all enrollment forms completed, signed, and turned in to Linda by the end of next Monday, December 17, 2008. This will allow us to process the enrollment and get everything submitted to the carriers on December 18. If this can be accomplished, there is a very good chance that everyone will receive their membership cards by January 1, 2009.

If you don't have your membership card by January 1 and you have an emergency or have an appointment scheduled prior to receipt, use the Temporary Information Cards found in your Health Plan Packet. You or your provider will be able to call Health Plan for your Group and personal ID numbers. If you have any questions regarding any information supplied in this memo or packet, please call or e-mail me.

WORKSHEET FOR ORGANIZING IDEAS—*Short Form*

SUBJECT: *Insurance Enrollment Forms Needed by December 17*

OPENING STATEMENT—*What information do you need to include?*

1 I. **Significance to the Readers**

    A. **What Prompts Your Document Now?** *2009 renewal rates for insurance increased 24%*

    B. **Importance of Subject:** *24% rate increase is too high for personnel and their families*

2 II. **Position:** *Therefore, I have put together a new benefits package with 9% average rate increase; Cafeteria contribution will increase from $425 to $490 to lessen impact*

7   A. **Essential Background:** *Packet: See spreadsheet comparing current vs. new benefits; use Temporary Card if necessary, or call for ID numbers; provider directories are in packet, at my desk, and online*

___   B. **Definition of Terms:** _____

   III. **Methodology (if necessary)**

3 A. **Sources of Data:** *I obtained quotes from several providers*

___ B. **Assumptions & Limitations:** _____

   IV. **Issues and Conclusions**

4, 8 ~~PRO~~	___ ~~CON~~
1. *24% rate increase is too high*	1. _____
2. *2009 plan offers more benefits*	2. _____
3. *How to change doctors*	3. _____
4. _____	4. _____
5. _____	5. _____

   V. **Recommendations**

5, 9 A. **Action Program:** *To receive membership cards by January 1, get enrollment forms to Linda by December 17; call or e-mail me if you have questions*

6   B. **Future Work:** *We will process forms and submit to carriers by December 18*

↑   *What is the best order in which to present your information?*

Medical Benefits Memo—Revised

Following is a solution to achieving the multiple purposes of this memo. First, separate out what you want people to do, from the justification for the changes, and from the changes themselves. Then give people a map of the detailed information that follows.

Notice that whereas the original memo is organized with headings that identify types of information—Premiums, Benefits, Provider Network, Summary Materials Enclosed—the rewrite focuses on action. The topic sentence of each of the first three paragraphs uses a verb that involves the reader in the decisions being made and the actions being requested—"Although I know none of us likes to change medical plans," "I obtained quotes from several different providers," "For everyone to receive their membership cards by January 1."

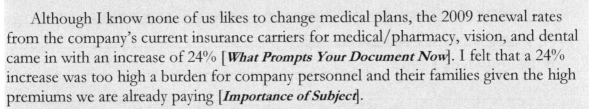

TO: All Employees
FROM: Office Manager
DATE: December 5, 2008
RE: Insurance Enrollment Forms Needed by December 17

Although I know none of us likes to change medical plans, the 2009 renewal rates from the company's current insurance carriers for medical/pharmacy, vision, and dental came in with an increase of 24% [**What Prompts Your Document Now**]. I felt that a 24% increase was too high a burden for company personnel and their families given the high premiums we are already paying [**Importance of Subject**].

Therefore, I obtained quotes from several providers [**Sources of Data**], and was able to put together a benefits package with rate increases averaging 9%. Although some items are difficult to compare, I believe the policies offered in 2009 represent an increase in benefits [**Position**]. To lessen the financial impact of the rate increase on families, the Cafeteria contributions for 2009 will only increase for each employee from $425 to $490 per month, or 15.3% [**Essential Background**].

For everyone to receive their membership cards by January 1, 2009, please complete, sign, and turn the enrollment forms to Linda by the end of the day, Monday, December 17, 2008 [**Action Program**]. This will enable us to process the enrollment and get everything submitted to the carriers on December 18 [**Future Work**].

Following is a summary of the materials in the enclosed packet and how to get coverage under the new benefits package.

Benefits are Compared in the Attached Information Packet

The contents of the enclosed information packet is summarized on the next page. Look in particular at the Comparison of Medical Benefits spreadsheet which compares our current benefits with those offered in 2009 [**Essential Background**].

What To Do Until You Get Your Membership Card

Use the Temporary Information Cards found in the enclosed Health Plan packet if you have an emergency or an appointment scheduled prior to receiving your membership card. You or your provider will be able to call Health Plan for your Group and personal ID numbers [**Essential Background**].

Finding or Getting Your Doctor in the Provider Network

In the enclosed Health Plan packet, you will also find Provider Directories for Vision and Alternative Care services. A larger directory of physicians is available at my desk. A complete listing can be found online at www.healthplan.com [*Essential Background*].

The network of providers is very extensive, which should reduce the need for individuals to change doctors. There are also procedures for including your physician in the network if he or she is not already a participant. Please let me know if this is an issue for you and I will help [*Issue*].

If you have any questions about the information in this memo or packet, please call or e-mail me [*Action Program*].

Summary of Enclosed Materials

Enrollment Forms, Stapled Together, Due to office December 17 by end of day

After reviewing the enclosed materials, please complete the following forms:

- Benefit Election & Payroll Deduction Authorization form – *BLUE SHEET*
- Health Plan Enrollment Form (Medical/Pharmacy/Vision Benefits)
  - On the top section, check the following boxes:
    - PPO
    - Open Enrollment
  - If you are declining, just complete the "Employee Information" and "I Decline" sections, and sign/date the form.
- Universal Health Care Enrollment Form (Dental)
  - To enroll, complete Sections A, B, C, D, F
  - To waive coverage, complete Sections A, E, F
- Adelphi Financial Group—Life Insurance Beneficiary Designation Form
  - All employees are automatically covered and need to complete this form.

Comparison of 2007 and 2008 Medical Benefits—YELLOW SHEET

- Employee Benefit Overview
- Group Number will be provided once all enrollment forms are submitted and processed.
- If all enrollment forms are submitted to the carrier by December 18, everyone will probably receive their membership cards by January 1.

Who Do I Call for Help?

- The PMK Group is our new Broker/Customer Service representative. They are the exclusive representatives for the Health Net Medical/Vision Plan we obtained through the Idaho Small Business Alliance Group.
- To give us only one point of contact, they are also servicing our Dental, Life, STD, and LTD Plans.
- You can contact them directly whenever you have questions about any of the policies.

Supplemental Materials

Health Plan Packet—Medical/Pharmacy/Vision Benefits
Universal Health Care Packet—Dental Coverage Outlined
Adelphi Financial Group
    Summary of Life and AD&D Insurance
    Summary of Short-Term Disability Insurance
    Summary of Long-Term Disability Insurance

The Courthouse Mystery Memo

The last example in this chapter is a tightly argued analysis of building codes and their legal requirements—so tightly argued, in fact, that it is difficult to tell what the author is trying to prove. Once again, this puzzle is largely the result of the author presenting information in the order in which he did his thinking.

In the end, the memo's purpose is only discovered by carefully reading the whole argument. In the middle of the document, in the last sentence of the eleventh paragraph is the solution to our mystery: "Since we are not increasing the projected area of the building, we have not changed the imposed demand on the structure, and no further evaluation of the building is required."

All that work to say that nothing more needs to be done?! Although one has to admire the author for his diligent commitment to the truth, there are more effective ways to present the results.

Furthermore, the argument does not end there. In the following paragraph the author explains why the analysis must continue: "While it is not mandatory under Appendix M that we evaluate or upgrade the existing structure, it is our professional opinion that it would be prudent to consider the effects of the added mass on the building."

And there lies the other problem with this otherwise masterful memo: weasel words, the unnecessary hedge. In addition to making the purpose of the memo explicit, the document needs a good edit. Read on and see how this maze of legalese was clarified through the use of plain English.

Mr. Frank Atkins
Bernalillo County Community Development Services
Albuquerque, NM 87101
RE: Bernalillo County Courthouse Reclad
Review No. BO-09-00271

Dear Frank:

This letter is in response to comment Note #2 in your plans correction notice dated May 27. Your note read as follows:

Please have the engineer verify, in a stamped letter, that all elements of the building remodel comply with all Sections of IBC Chapter 34.

- *Verify that all additions and/or alterations to the existing structure have been evaluated and shall not increase the force in any structural element by more than 5 percent, unless the increased forces on the element are still in compliance with the code for new structures IBC Section 3403.2.*
- *Verify that all additions and/or alterations have been evaluated for both wind and seismic forces and found to meet the requirements of all structural sections of the IBC and ASCE 7-05.*

We understand that Bob Vinton of Vinton Architects previously discussed with you our intent to base our design on Appendix M of the New Mexico State Building Code (NMSBC). Appendix M recognizes the 2006 International Existing Building Code (IEBC) as a valid code alternate where accepted by the authority having jurisdiction.

Under Appendix M of the NMSBC, this project would be considered a Level 2 Alteration because it meets the criteria for a Level 2 Alteration as defined by Section 404.1 of the IEBC (the project includes the elimination of some windows) while falling short of the criteria to be considered a Level 3 Alteration as defined by the amendment to Section 405.1 in Appendix M (we are modifying less than 50% of the floor area of the building.)

Since this is a Level 2 Alteration, Section 404.2 of the IEBC requires compliance with the provisions of Chapter 6 and 7 of the IEBC. The requirements for seismic loads are found in Section 707.4.2 of the IEBC, which reads as follows:

707.4.2 Lateral loads. *Buildings in which Level 2 alterations increase the seismic base shear by more than 10 percent or decrease the seismic base shear capacity by more than 10 percent shall comply with the structural requirements specified in Sections 807.5 and 807.7. Changes in base shear and base shear capacity shall be calculated relative to conditions at the time of the original construction.*

While we are not decreasing the base shear capacity of the existing structure, we are potentially increasing the building mass by more than 10%. If this is the case, we would need to comply with Section 807.5 of Appendix M. The requirements of Section 807.5 depend on whether the work is considered a substantial improvement. Section 202 of Appendix M defines a substantial improvement as follows:

Substantial Improvement. *For the purpose of determining compliance with the flood provisions of this code, any repair, alteration, addition, or improvement of a building or structure, the cost of which equals or exceeds 50 percent of the market value of the structure, before the improvement or repair is started.*

One odd thing about this amendment in Appendix M is that it states that it carries over from the IEBC the phrase "for the purpose of determining compliance with the flood provisions of this code." This is odd because elsewhere in Appendix M, amendments are made to the seismic provisions of the IEBC that make reference to substantial improvements. It is our interpretation that the above definition of substantial improvement is intended to apply to all references to substantial improvement in Appendix M. Assuming our interpretation is correct, this project would not be classified as a substantial improvement as the project cost is less than 50% of the market value of the structure. This means that our project has to comply with Section 807.5.3 of Appendix M:

807.5.3 Limited structural alteration. *Where any building undergoes less than substantial improvement, the evaluation and analysis shall demonstrate that the altered building or structure complies with the loads applicable at the time the building was constructed.*

At the time this building was constructed, there were no seismic design requirements in the building code; lateral design was based on a flat 20 psf wind load. Under Section 807.5.3, this 20 psf wind load is all we need to consider. Since we are not increasing the projected area of the building, we have not changed the imposed demand on the structure, and no further evaluation of the building is required.

While it is not mandatory under Appendix M that we evaluate or upgrade the existing structure, it is our professional opinion that it would be prudent to consider the effects of the added mass on the building.

The new brick cladding only relies on the existing structure for stability in the out-of-plane direction; the wall has been designed to cantilever from the foundations to resist the in-plane seismic loads.

The lateral force resisting system for both of the wings in the direction perpendicular to the new brick cladding consists of 7", cast-in-place concrete shear walls. Our calculations show that these walls are lightly loaded, even using the 2006 IBC response spectra and the additional mass of the new cladding. Using an R of five for an ordinary concrete wall, the resulting ultimate shear stress is not more than 20 psi.

Since the walls appear to have sufficient capacity, the only remaining concern is whether the diaphragms have sufficient capacity to deliver the loads to the shear walls. The south wing is two levels, with a slab-on-form deck floor at the floor level, and steel roof deck at the roof level. The east wing is a single level, with steel roof deck at the roof level. Both the floors and roofs are supported by steel joists spanning perpendicular to the new brick cladding. At the perimeter of the building, the joists bear on top of steel wide flange girders. While it is possible the roof deck diaphragm is supplemented by horizontal steel rod bracing similar to what we observed in the penthouse, we have been unable to find documentation to verify that. As a result we have assumed that the steel roof deck provides the only diaphragm load path at the roof level.

It appears to us that the weakest link in the diaphragm system is the apparent lack of a chord for the roof deck diaphragm. While the perimeter beams have the potential to act as a chord, there appears to be no direct connection between the roof deck and the perimeter beam because the two are separated from each other by the depth of the joist seat. To address this deficiency, we are adding angles to create a load path from the steel roof deck to the perimeter roof beam. These angles are shown on sections E and E1 on sheet S204 of our drawing set.

If you have any questions on this matter, I can be reached by telephone at 503-296-0343 or by email at dan.jones@rbceng.com.

Yours truly,

WORKSHEET FOR ORGANIZING IDEAS—*Short Form*

SUBJECT: _Bernalillo County Courthouse Reclad Complies with Building Codes_

OPENING STATEMENT—*What information do you need to include?*

_1_ I. Significance to the Readers

    A. What Prompts Your Document Now? _Note #2 in your plans correction, May 27_

    _____

    B. Importance of Subject: _____

    _____

_2_ II. Position: _Reclad complies with all sections of IBC Chapter 34_

    _____

__   **A. Essential Background:** _____

    _____

__   **B. Definition of Terms:** _____

    _____

III. Methodology (if necessary)

__ **A. Sources of Data:** _____

    _____

__ **B. Assumptions & Limitations:** _____

    _____

IV. Issues and Conclusions

_3_ PRO   **__ ~~CON~~**

    1. _Complies with NMSBC Appendix M_   **1.** _Max shear stress not >20 psi, load at const time_

    2. _Complies with 2006 IEBC_   **2.** _Adding angles to roof deck diaphragm_

    3. _Meets wind & seismic requirements_   **3.** _____

    4. _Complies with loads at time of const_   **4.** _____

    5. _No seismic req at time of const._   **5.** _____

V. Recommendations

_4_ A. Action Program: _If you have questions, call or e-mail me_

    _____

_5_ B. Future Work: _Adding angles on sheet S204, sec E/E1 to strengthen roof deck_
    diaphragm.

↑ *What is the best order in which to present your information?*

The Courthouse Mystery Memo—Revised

To plan a document of this complexity would, of course, require more than the Short Form of the *Worksheet for Organizing Ideas*. Each of the Conclusions outlined in the Opening Statement below needs to be substantiated through discussion of the applicable building codes, as the author has done. To outline such a detailed argument would require the *Worksheet for Organizing Ideas—Long Form*.

Nonetheless, by outlining the letter on a *Worksheet—Short Form*, we have extracted the Position and the arguments that support it. In addition, by applying the Principles for Paragraphs and Sentences explained in *Organizing Ideas*, we have simplified the sentence and paragraph structure throughout to make it all more readable. And we have added sideheadings to the attachment to signal the principal elements of the discussion.

Mr. Frank Atkins
Bernalillo County Community Development Services
Albuquerque, NM 87101
RE: Bernalillo County Courthouse Reclad Complies with Building Codes
Review No. BO-09-00271

Dear Frank:

In response to your request in Note #2 in the plans correction notice dated May 27, RBC Engineering verifies that all elements of the Bernalillo County Courthouse remodel comply with all Sections of IBC Chapter 34 [**What Prompts Your Document Now**].

Specifically, RBC Engineering certifies that [**Position**]:

- The Bernalillo County Courthouse Reclad complies with all Sections of Appendix M of the New Mexico State Building Code (NMSBC) and the 2006 International Existing Building Code (IEBC), and
- All alterations have been evaluated for both wind and seismic forces and meet the requirements of the IEBC and ASCE 7-05.

Briefly stated, our certification is based on the following considerations [**Conclusions**]. A complete justification of our evaluation is included in the attachment.

1. Our design is based on Appendix M of the New Mexico State Building Code (NMSBC), which recognizes the 2006 International Existing Building Code (IEBC) as a valid code alternate.
2. Under Section 807.5.3 of Appendix M, it is only necessary to demonstrate that the project *"complies with the loads applicable at the time the building was constructed."*
3. When the building was constructed, there were no seismic design requirements in the building code. Lateral design was based on a flat 20 psf wind load.

Therefore, no further evaluation of the building is required, since we are not increasing the projected area of the building, and we have not changed the imposed demand on the structure.

Although evaluating or upgrading the existing structure is not mandatory under Appendix M, we took the extra precaution of evaluating the brick wall in terms of its adding mass to the building. Our calculations show that the maximum shear stress of the brick wall is not more than 20 psi, the load that was applicable at the time the building was built [**Conclusion**].

The only remaining concern is whether the diaphragms have sufficient capacity to deliver the loads to the shear walls. The weakest link in the diaphragm system appears to be the apparent lack of a chord for the roof deck diaphragm. To address this deficiency, we are adding angles, shown on sections E and E1 on sheet S204 of our drawing set, to create a load path from the steel roof deck to the perimeter roof beam [***Conclusions***].

If you have any questions, please call me at 503-296-0343 or email me at dan.jones@rbceng.com [***Action Program***].

Yours truly,

Attachment—

Bernalillo County Courthouse Reclad Compliance with Building Codes

Following is a complete explanation of RBC Engineering's certification that the brick reclad of the Bernalillo County Courthouse complies with all Sections of Appendix M of the New Mexico State Building Code (NMSBC) and the 2006 International Existing Building Code (IEBC).

This certification is submitted in response to Note #2 in the Bernalillo County Community Development Services plans correction notice, dated May 27, 2008, which reads:

> *Please have the engineer verify, in a stamped letter, that all elements of the building remodel comply with all Sections of IBC Chapter 34.*
> - *Verify that all additions and/or alterations to the existing structure have been evaluated and shall not increase the force in any structural element by more than 5 percent, unless the increased forces on the element are still in compliance with the code for new structures IBC Section 3403.2.*
> - *Verify that all additions and/or alterations have been evaluated for both wind and seismic forces and found to meet the requirements of all structural section of the IBC and ASCE 7-05.*

As explained below, our summary assessment is that under New Mexico State Building Code (NMSBC) Appendix M, Section 807.5.3, a 20 psf wind-load is all we need to consider in evaluating whether the building complies with the NMSBC and the International Existing Building Code (IEBC).

Since we are not increasing the projected area of the building, we have not changed the imposed demand on the structure, and no further evaluation of the building is required by the code.

Furthermore, additional consideration of the effect of brick cladding on the building does not change our evaluation that the walls have sufficient capacity. As a precaution, however, we have added angles, shown on sections E and E1 on sheet S204 of our drawing set, to ensure that the diaphragms have sufficient capacity to deliver the loads to the shear walls.

Our reasoning for these conclusions is as follows.

Analysis of New Mexico State Building Code Appendix M

As Bob Vinton of Vinton Architects previously discussed with Bernalillo County Community Development Services, RBC Engineering's intent is to base our design on Appendix M of the New Mexico State Building Code (NMSBC). Appendix M recognizes the 2006 International Existing Building Code (IEBC) as a valid code alternate where accepted by the authority having jurisdiction.

Under Appendix M of the NMSBC, this project would be considered a Level 2 Alteration as defined by Section 404.1 of the IEBC, because the project includes the elimination of some windows, and falls short of the criteria for a Level 3 Alteration as defined by the amendment to Appendix M, Section 405.1 because we are modifying less than 50% of the floor area of the building.

As a Level 2 Alteration, Section 404.2 of the IEBC requires compliance with the provisions of Chapter 6 and 7 of the IEBC. The requirements for seismic loads are found in the IEBC, Section 707.4.2, which reads:

707.4.2 Lateral loads. Buildings in which Level 2 alterations increase the seismic base shear by more than 10 percent or decrease the seismic base shear capacity by more than 10 percent shall comply with the structural requirements specified in Sections 807.5 and 807.7. Changes in base shear and base shear capacity shall be calculated relative to conditions at the time of the original construction.

While we are not decreasing the base shear capacity of the existing structure, we are potentially increasing the building mass by more than 10%. If this is the case, we need to comply with Appendix M, Section 807.5. The requirements of Section 807.5 depend on whether the work is considered a substantial improvement. Section 202 of Appendix M defines a substantial improvement as follows:

Substantial Improvement. For the purpose of determining compliance with the flood provisions of this code, any repair, alteration, addition, or improvement of a building or structure, the cost of which equals or exceeds 50 percent of the market value of the structure, before the improvement or repair is started.

We interpret the above definition of substantial improvement as applying to all references to substantial improvement in Appendix M because, although this amendment to Appendix M includes the phrase *"For the purpose of determining compliance with the flood provisions of this code"* from the IEBC, amendments to the seismic provisions of the IEBC elsewhere in Appendix M also refer to "substantial improvements."

Assuming our interpretation is correct, the Bernalillo County Courthouse project would not be classified as a substantial improvement because the project cost is less than 50% of the market value of the structure.

This means that our project must comply with Section 807.5.3 of Appendix M:

807.5.3 Limited structural alteration. Where any building undergoes less than substantial improvement, the evaluation and analysis shall demonstrate that the altered building or structure complies with the loads applicable at the time the building was constructed.

Wind Load as the Basis for Evaluation

At the time the courthouse building was constructed, there were no seismic design requirements in the building code. Lateral design was based on a flat 20 psf wind load.

Therefore, under Section 807.5.3, a 20 psf wind-load is all we need to determine whether the building complies with the New Mexico State Building Code and the International Existing Building Code.

Since we are not increasing the projected area of the building, we have not changed the imposed demand on the structure, and no further evaluation of the building is required.

Effects of Brick Cladding on the Building

While it is not mandatory under Appendix M that we evaluate or upgrade the existing structure, we have considered it advisable to evaluate the effects of the added mass of the brick cladding on the building.

The new brick cladding only relies on the existing structure for stability in the out-of-plane direction; the wall has been designed to cantilever from the foundations to resist the in-plane seismic loads.

The lateral force resisting system for both of the wings in the direction perpendicular to the new brick cladding consists of 7", cast-in-place concrete shear walls. Our calculations show that these walls are lightly loaded, even using the 2006 IBC response spectra and the additional mass of the new cladding. Using an R of five for an ordinary concrete wall, the resulting ultimate shear stress is not more than 20 psi.

Strengthening the Roof Deck Diaphragm

Since the walls appear to have sufficient capacity, the only remaining concern is whether the diaphragms have sufficient capacity to deliver the loads to the shear walls.

The weakest link in the diaphragm system appears to be the apparent lack of a chord for the roof deck diaphragm. While the perimeter beams have the potential to act as a chord, there appears to be no direct connection between the roof deck and the perimeter beam because the two are separated from each other by the depth of the joist seat.

To address this deficiency, we are adding angles to create a load path from the steel roof deck to the perimeter roof beam. These angles are shown on sections E and E1 on sheet S204 of our drawing set.

The south wing is two levels, with a slab-on-form deck floor at the floor level, and steel roof deck at the roof level. The east wing is a single level, with steel roof deck at the roof level. Both the floors and roofs are supported by steel joists spanning perpendicular to the new brick cladding. At the perimeter of the building, the joists bear on top of steel wide flange girders.

While it is possible that the roof deck diaphragm is supplemented by horizontal steel rod bracing similar to what we observed in the penthouse, we have been unable to find documentation to verify that. As a result we have assumed that the steel roof deck provides the only diaphragm load path at the roof level.

One effect of the revision is that the new version is quite a bit longer. This is primarily the result of adding an Opening Statement and breaking the long paragraphs into shorter ones throughout. The benefit, however, is that the argument is more readable and easier to follow.

3. The "One-Page Memo with Attachments"

S OME OF THE EXAMPLES WE HAVE SEEN ON THE PRECEDING PAGES are one- or two-page documents that consist of just an Opening Statement. Ensuring the readers get all the information in such correspondence is relatively simple because there is limited detail to be presented.

In correspondence of more than two pages, however, readers may be overwhelmed by the number of pages and not have the time or patience to read the entire document. Writing a Summing Up for longer documents is also considered one of the more difficult tasks in business writing, because it is difficult to restate the Position and recap the primary Conclusions and Recommendations without simply repeating what was already stated in the Opening Statement.

A simpler approach to presenting information in the Body of a longer document is the "one-page memo with attachments" format. When using this format, it is assumed that the reader will only read those sections of the attachment that contain information that is important to them. In this case, a Summing Up is not necessary, because the document will only be read selectively, rather than all the way through. In this regard, a "one-page memo with attachments" is simpler to read and simpler to write.

Following is an example of a long narrative proposal that is revised as a one-page memo with an attachment. More examples of proposals are presented in Chapter 4.

A Long Narrative Proposal

In the four-page letter presented next, you will see a classic format used by consultants to present an account of the work to be performed for the reader, a client. The format presents the information in the order in which the writer did her thinking as opposed to the order in which the reader wants the information. Then you will see a reformatted account of the same letter consisting of a one-page summary followed by a four-page attachment.

The original letter begins with standard opening paragraph, which thanks the reader in a perfunctory fashion for the "opportunity" and mentions the "primary objectives." Then the author launches into a detailed account of **Our Understanding.** No new information is presented here for the prospective client—just a rehash of what the client has said he wants. It is not the essential reading that its placement suggests. It is better left to an attachment, where the reader can find it if necessary.

For that matter, **Project Scope** is not critical information either. It seems to be a further account of information the reader already knows. Again, it should be relegated to an attachment.

Project Approach gets to the heart of this correspondence. Here the author sets forth the phases in which the project will be performed and what the client will get in each phase. This definitely belongs earlier in the letter.

As usual in all correspondence sent to clients, the fees are whispered at the end: "We estimate this project will require approximately 500 hours, . . . [which] equates to a discounted professional fee of about $68,000." I suspect 90 percent of readers glance at the first page of such correspondence, then immediately jump to the end to find out the cost—which incidentally is couched in a weasel-worded way. And "estimated at approximately" is certainly a doublet, since an estimate is, by definition, approximate.

The fact that the fees are buried suggests the author hopes to make the cost more palatable to the reader by presenting an extensive account of what the consultant will do and what the client will get. Don't count on it, primarily because the client is not likely to read the proposal in the order in which the information is presented. Be confident in the value of your services and state the fees on the first page. And if the fees are discounted, spell out by how much.

Also, the term "out of pocket" expenses always raises a red flag for me. How much will these represent?

One final question: what is the Position? Is there one hidden in the middle of the ***Project Approach?*** Or implied in the account of ***Our Understanding?*** If only the writer could conceal the expenses as effectively.

Dear Mr. Tatum:

We appreciate the opportunity to provide network and telecommunications assistance to the Tatum Alliance. This letter identifies consulting services Cole Consulting Group (CCG) will provide to you during this engagement. As we discussed yesterday, your two primary objectives of this engagement are to (1) better understand network technology and (2) develop a plan for the future network infrastructure for Tatum Alliance.

Our Understanding

During our discussion last Thursday with you and Sally, you identified several issues that you would like to address. Following are your current issues.

- Tatum Alliance is in the process of preparing a corporate-wide strategic information systems plan. The network plan should be coordinated with the strategic plan. An advisory group composed of management should be involved throughout both planning projects.
- There is currently a severe shortage of telephone and data cable to certain areas of your affiliated operations. As new cable is installed, there appears to be a need to install fiber optic cable to support a high-speed network. This network should be able to support voice, data, image, and video in the future.
- There are several existing local area networks. However, format hardware and software standards have not been established for client-server computing.
- Tatum Alliance is beginning to explore the possibility of remote and intercampus image transfer. There is a need to establish communications standards for clinical imaging equipment to be used during evaluation and purchase of equipment.

To address these issues, you have identified a project scope you would like CCG's assistance in performing.

Project Scope

CCG will use our network methodology to organize and address the issues you have identified. We have developed a project approach we believe addresses the following topics in a logical manner.

- Conduct detailed educational sessions with the Information Services and Telecom directors of Tatum Alliance on Local Area Network, Wide Area Network, and Client Server concepts, terminology, and components.
- Meet with a management task force regularly during the project to educate them on the technology and enlist them as champions of the concept.
- Review the alternative local area network technologies and assist you in developing standards for Tatum Alliance for cable, network interface cards, network hubs, workstations, etc.
- Assist you in developing a network architecture that is consistent with Tatum Alliance strategic information systems plan.
- Assist you in developing a Premises Distribution System (copper and fiber-optics-based) that can be implemented in phases over a period of time.
- Provide you with limited assistance in education and evaluation of other specific technologies (e.g., video, e-mail, office automation software, etc.).

Project Approach

We believe this project should be approached in four phases. Following are a summary of each phase and a description of deliverables. Attached is a detailed workplan for your review.

Phase I   Conduct Network Education

During this phase we will spend two to three days educating you and Sally on the fundamentals of networking: cable, network topologies, network operating systems, presentation and session control, and finally application layer communication. We will provide you with materials on each topic that you can refer to later.

In a follow-up session, we will discuss alternative hardware technologies for personal computer workstations, network servers, network interface cards, intelligent wiring hubs, bridges, routers, and gateways. After these discussions, you will be prepared to discuss a network architecture and make informed decisions regarding Tatum Alliance network standards during Phases II, III, and IV of the project.

Deliverables from Phase I:

- Network components seminar notes.
- Network technologies seminar notes.

Phase II   Develop a Network Architecture

During this phase we will assist you in developing a high-level network architecture which addresses standards for technology, hardware, cable, software, management, and support. The architecture should support your long-term objectives for corporate-wide computing and this will be the time to evaluate the impact on the information systems organization.

We will prepare recommendations regarding the network architecture for Tatum Alliance. Using the information learned in Phase I, you will be able to make informed decisions regarding the most appropriate network architecture for Tatum Alliance.

Once we have agreed to network architecture, we will prepare a strategy document to support the architecture. The strategy will address computing technology, hardware, software, and organizational components of the strategy.

Deliverables from Phase II:

- Network architecture recommendations.
- Final statement of network architecture.
- High-level strategy document.
- Priorities and implementation schedule.

Phase III Design the Campus Network

Phase III will be used to design the physical infrastructure necessary to support the network architecture and strategy. We will recommend a design based upon our understanding of Tatum Alliance's current and future requirements. We will then develop a detailed cable design for your affiliated operations. Tatum Alliance will then be able to use the infrastructure over a period of time.

Deliverables from Phase III:

- Physical cable standards.
- Backbone cable design, including cable sizes, types, closet locations, etc.
- Intermediate distribution closet standards (e.g., size, HVAC, etc.).

Phase IV Develop Network Component Standards

During this phase CCG will review Tatum Alliance's strategic information services plan and develop standards for networking technologies, including workstations, servers, interface cards, hubs, etc., to support the long-term goals and objectives. These standards will encompass the primary components for enterprise-wide networking. Other technologies that you need assistance with will be identified, prioritized, and addressed (e.g., video conferencing, medical imaging, etc.).

Deliverables from Phase IV:

- Draft of standards for network components.
- Final standards for network components.
- Memos addressing related technologies.

We will meet with you regularly during the project to review project progress.

Project Staffing, Timing, and Fees

Staffing

Ben Goodman, a senior manager in our Atlanta office, will work with you on this project (résumé attached). Ben will assign additional staff specialists to assist him as required. Other consultants may include Lionel Hampton to assist with network component education, and Dudley Brooks who has worked on similar standards development projects.

Timing

Based on our knowledge of the project at this time, we estimate the time to complete each phase as follows:

Phase I	2 weeks
Phase II	4 weeks
Phase III	6 weeks
Phase IV	8 weeks

Total elapsed time will be approximately three to four months, since Phases III and IV will overlap.

Fees

We estimate this project will require approximately 500 hours of professional time. This equates to a fee of about $68,000. Out-of-pocket expenses such as secretarial support, mileage, and other related expenses will be billed at actual cost. Invoices are payable upon receipt. Should the level of effort or project scope change, we would notify you and gain your concurrence prior to incurring any unplanned fee or expense.

We are prepared to begin this project on October 23 with a seminar on networking components. We look forward to continuing our relationship with Tatum Alliance. Should you have any questions concerning our proposal, please call me or Ben Goodman at (404) 123-4567. We are looking forward to working with you on this important project.

Very truly yours,

A Long Narrative Proposal—Revised

What follows is a cut-and-paste revision of the original letter. The important information appears on the first page and Attachment 1 presents the workplan, which has been omitted for the purpose of this example. Finally, Attachment 2 provides the details of ***Our Understanding***, ***Project Scope***, and so forth. The structure of a one-page summary followed by details in an attachment is easier to follow than the original four-page account.

Arthur Tatum, because he is a busy CEO, may choose to read just the first page for an overview and then pass the document on to his manager of Information Services. She will read the first page and then study the attachments for the details she needs to perform her job.

Another change that makes this letter more readable is the presence of a Position, which serves as the unifying proposition. All the other information expands on that Position.

Three other changes deserve mention. First, the projected costs of the work are stated on the first page, right after the deliverables. Let's be forthright about this matter. After all, readers are going to look for this information, so we should make it easier for them to find.

Second, the next-to-last paragraph of the Opening Statement provides a summary of the areas covered in the attachment so the readers have a table of contents for what appears in the pages that follow.

Third, the use of the Latin abbreviations ***i.e.*** and ***e.g.*** has been eliminated. They are too academic for business writing and are often used interchangeably, which is not correct.

Instead of *i.e.* use its English equivalent of *that is*. For **e.g.** substitute *for example* or *such as*. Instances of *etc.* have also been eliminated—its use is just a lazy way to complete a list. If there are more items to include, list them. If there aren't, leave the list as it is.

The following revision demonstrates why readers prefer a one-page document with five or ten pages in an attachment to a three-page document—they get the key information up front.

Dear Mr. Tatum:

Cole Consulting Group (CCG) is looking forward to providing network and telecommunications assistance to the Tatum Alliance. This letter identifies consulting services CCG will provide to you during this engagement [**What Prompts Your Document Now**].

As we discussed yesterday, your two primary objectives of this engagement are to (1) better understand network technology and (2) develop a plan for the future network infrastructure for Tatum Alliance [**Background and Importance of Subject**].

We propose to perform this project in four phases [**Position**] and we are prepared to begin Phase I on October 23 with a seminar on networking components [**Future Work**]. Following are a summary of each phase, its expected duration, and a brief list of deliverables. Attachment 1 provides a detailed workplan.

Phase I Conduct Network Education (2 weeks)

- Network components seminar notes.
- Network technologies seminar notes. [**Issues**]

Phase II Develop a Network Architecture (4 weeks)

- Network architecture recommendations.
- Final statement of network architecture.
- High-level strategy document.
- Priorities and implementation schedule. [**Issues**]

Phase III Design the Campus Network (6 weeks)

- Physical cable standards.
- Backbone cable design, including cable sizes, types, closet locations, etc.
- Intermediate distribution closet standards (e.g., size, HVAC, etc.). [**Issues**]

Phase IV Develop Network Component Standards (8 weeks)

- Draft of standards for network components.
- Final standards for network components.
- Memos addressing related technologies. [**Issues**]

This project will require approximately 500 hours of professional time. This equates to a fee of $68,000. Total time for the project will be three to four months [**Conclusions**].

In Attachment 2 you will find an account of (1) our understanding of your needs, (2) the project scope, (3) our project approach in more detail, and (4) a further account of staffing, timing, and fees [**Further Issues**].

Ben Goodman of our Atlanta office will work with you on this project. We look forward to seeing you on October 23 [**Future Work**]. In the meantime, please call Ben or me at (404) 123-4567 if you have any questions [***Action Program***].

Very truly yours,

Attachments

Attachment 2—Project Proposal

Below is an account of (1) our understanding of your needs, (2) the project scope, (3) our project approach in more detail, and (4) staffing, timing, and fees.

Our Understanding

During our discussion last Thursday with you and Sally, you identified several issues that you would like to address. Following are your current issues.

- **Tatum Alliance's corporate-wide strategic information systems plan.** The network plan should be coordinated with the strategic plan. An advisory group composed of management should be involved throughout both planning projects.
- **A severe shortage of telephone and data cable in certain areas** of your affiliated operations. As new cable is installed, there appears to be a need to install fiber optic cable to support a high-speed network. This network should be able to support voice, data, image, and video in the future.
- **Existing local area networks**. Hardware and software standards need to be established for client-server computing.
- **Remote and intercampus image transfer.** Communications standards need to be established for clinical imaging equipment to be used during evaluation and purchase of equipment.

To address these issues, you have identified a project scope you would like CCG's assistance in performing.

Project Scope

CCG will to use our network methodology to organize and address the issues you have identified. We have developed a project approach we believe addresses the following topics in a logical manner.

- **Conduct detailed education sessions** with the Information Services and Telecom directors of Tatum Alliance on Local Area Network, Wide Area Network, and Client Server concepts, terminology, and components.
- **Meet regularly with a management task force** to educate them on the technology and enlist them as champions of the concept.
- **Review alternative local area network technologies** and assist in developing standards for Tatum Alliance for cable, network interface cards, network hubs, workstations, etc.
- **Assist in developing a network architecture** that is consistent with Tatum Alliance strategic information systems plan.
- **Assist in developing a Premises Distribution System** (copper and fiber-optics-based) that can be implemented in phases over a period of time.
- **Provide limited assistance in education and evaluation of other specific technologies** (e.g., video, e-mail, office automation software, etc.).

Project Approach

We believe this project should be approached in four phases. Following are a summary of each phase and a description of deliverables. A detailed workplan is also attached for your review.

Phase I   Conduct Network Education

During this phase we will spend two to three days educating you and Sally on the fundamentals of networking: cable, network topologies, network operating systems, presentation and session control, and finally application layer communication. We will provide you with materials on each topic that you can refer to later.

In a follow-up session, we will discuss alternative hardware technologies for personal computer workstations, network servers, network interface cards, intelligent wiring hubs, bridges, routers, and gateways. After these discussions you will be prepared to discuss a network architecture and make informed decisions regarding Tatum Alliance network standards during Phases II, III, and IV of the project.

Deliverables from Phase I:

- Network components seminar notes.
- Network technologies seminar notes.

Phase II   Develop a Network Architecture

During this phase we will assist you in developing a high-level network architecture that addresses standards for technology, hardware, cable, software, management, and support. The architecture should support your long-term objectives for corporate-wide computing, and this will be the time to evaluate the impact on the information systems organization.

We will prepare recommendations regarding the network architecture for Tatum Alliance. Using the information learned in Phase I, you will be able to make informed decisions regarding the most appropriate network architecture for Tatum Alliance.

Once we have agreed on network architecture, we will prepare a strategy document to support the architecture. The strategy will address computing technology, hardware, software, and organizational components of the strategy.

Deliverables from Phase II:

- Network architecture recommendations.
- Final statement of network architecture.
- High-level strategy document.
- Priorities and implementation schedule.

Phase III   Design the Campus Network

Phase III will be used to design the physical infrastructure necessary to support the network architecture and strategy. We will recommend a design based upon our understanding of Tatum Alliance's current and future requirements. We will then develop a detailed cable design for your affiliated operations. Tatum Alliance will then be able to use the design to bid components of the design, allowing you to build the infrastructure over a period of time.

Deliverables from Phase III:

- Physical cable standards.
- Backbone cable design, including cable sizes, types, closet locations, etc.
- Intermediate distribution closet standards (e.g., size, HVAC, etc.).

Phase IV Develop Network Component Standards

During this phase CCG will review Tatum Alliance's strategic information services plan and develop standards for networking technologies, including workstations, servers, interface cards, hubs, etc., to support the long-term goals and objectives. These standards will encompass the primary components for enterprise-wide networking. Other technologies that you need assistance with will be identified, prioritized, and addressed (such as video conferencing and medical imaging).

Deliverables from Phase IV:

- Draft of standards for network components.
- Final standards for network components.
- Memos addressing related technologies. [*Issues*]

We will meet with you regularly during the project to review project progress.

Project Staffing, Timing, and Fees

Staffing

As I noted above, Ben Goodman, a senior manager in our Atlanta office will work with you on this project (résumé attached). Ben will assign additional staff specialists to assist him as required. Other consultants may include Lionel Hampton to assist with network component education, and Dudley Brooks who has worked on similar standards development projects.

Timing

Based on our knowledge of the project at this time, we estimate the time to complete each phase as follows:

Phase I	2 weeks
Phase II	4 weeks
Phase III	6 weeks
Phase IV	8 weeks

Total elapsed time will be approximately three to four months, since Phases III and IV will overlap.

Fees

As I mentioned in our cover letter, this project will require approximately 500 hours of professional time for a total professional fee of $68,000. Out-of-pocket expenses such as secretarial support, mileage, and other related expenses will be billed at actual cost and will not exceed 7 percent of the total billable costs. Invoices are payable upon receipt. If the level of effort or project scope should change, we will notify you and obtain your agreement prior to incurring any unplanned fee or expense.

4. Persuasive Proposals

A WELL-WRITTEN PROPOSAL IS HARD TO FIND. TOO OFTEN, proposals are just a haphazard collection of information, loosely organized to establish the qualifications of a product, company, or professional firm. For some reason, people commonly fail to actually advocate for their products or services in proposals. They just present their information without making an effective argument for why readers should buy the product or service.

The most likely explanation for this weakness is that people don't want to be perceived as crude salespeople. So how does one sell or advocate for what one has to offer without sounding crass? What does professional salesmanship look like?

The approach explained in *Organizing Ideas* provides a starting point for constructing a professional sales presentation. Begin by telling your readers why you are writing—*Thank you for your interest in our services… The following document outlines our proposal to…* Then make your case: *We believe that our products/services are the finest available for the following three reasons…* And so on.

Although the *Spence & Company* approach provides an effective way to persuade your readers to take action or accept a certain idea, the actual arguments you organize into the basic structure are what determine whether your proposal will have the impact that you intend.

Let's look at some examples of the elements of a persuasive proposal.

A "Shoulder-to-Shoulder" Pitch

The first example is well-structured but the content is weak.

Although "We are pleased to submit our proposal to…" is a common beginning for proposals, it is inherently unprofessional because it expresses false enthusiasm. Simply saying "Attached is our proposal" is no more inspired, but at least it eliminates the insincerity of "We are pleased." Considering the last-minute work that goes into many proposals, "We are relieved to submit our proposal" is more frequently the case. Given that such a beginning would obviously be too candid, how about "Thank you for asking Rouse Consulting to submit the attached proposal to develop…?"

The second paragraph is an effective summary of the sections in the attached proposal. While the sections are not unusual, the summary of these topics at the beginning does something most proposals don't do which is to give the reader a map of the details that follow and where to find the information they are most interested in.

From there, however, the proposal becomes progressively less persuasive. Where is the Position? Although it can be inferred in the sentence that reads "The following points summarize specific reasons why we are particularly well-qualified to assist Ellington

Electronics with this project," the emphasis here falls on "The following points summarize specific reasons…", rather than on the idea that Ellington Electronics is well-qualified for the project.

To make the Position stand out, we should rework the sentence to read "We are particularly well-qualified to assist Ellington Electronics with this project based on five factors."

The reasons that follow don't deliver on their promise to establish the qualifications of the firm making the proposal. The first sideheading—**Experience with Sales Forecasting and Distribution Resource Planning (DRP) Systems**—sounds good, but the two sentences beneath the sideheading basically say that the firm has the experience because, well, because it has the experience. There is no support for the claim of experience. What is needed is a brief account of two or three engagements performed in the past year that are similar to the work Ellington needs.

The next qualification says the same thing: "We have the background because we have the background." By the fourth bullet, the author has run out of the usual qualifications and resorts to the claim that the firm offers a "shoulder-to-shoulder" approach, which is just empty, feel-good nonsense. In fact, the whole sentence is meaningless. "Our 'shoulder-to-shoulder' approach permits us to function as a catalyst to the project team." What does that mean?

The last bullet returns to the qualification of experience raised in the first point in the list, but, again, without evidence to support it. The sideheading claims "**Large Scale System Development and Implementation Experience**." Is the claim substantiated? Not at all. The first sentence after the sideheading reads, "We will draw upon our experience . . . ." and the next sentence echoes that notion: "We will bring the practical experience . . . ." What experience? Where? For what client? When?

The last paragraph concludes the proposal on a weak Assumption: "We trust this proposal conveys our enthusiasm for assisting you and Ellington Electronics with this important first stage of the project." You haven't proved that to me. No wonder the fee of $134,000 is not mentioned until the last line on page 17 of the attached proposal.

The lesson to be learned from this example is that good structure is useless if it does not present effective arguments.

Mr. William Strayhorn
Ellington Electronics
111 Avenue A
New York, NY 10000

Dear Mr. Strayhorn:

We are pleased to submit our proposal to assist Ellington Electronics, Inc. with the Distribution Resource Planning (DRP) project [***What Prompts Your Document Now***]. We are eager to work with you and your staff in this very important first stage of the project [***Importance of Subject***].

As a follow-up to our discussion we have organized our proposal as follows:

I. Understanding of the Project
II. Garner Associates Approach
III. Organization and Staffing
IV. Timing, Level of Effort, and Professional Fees [***Issues***].

The following points summarize specific reasons why we are particularly well qualified to assist Ellington Electronics with this project [***Position***].

- **Experience with Sales Forecasting and Distribution Resource Planning (DRP) Systems** [***Issue***]—We have hands-on experience with sales forecasting and DRP systems. Our experience will help expedite the formulation of a business systems model tailored for sales forecasting and DRP at Ellington [***Conclusion and Data***].

- **Significant Background with Ellington Electronics' Systems Environment (OSB and MRP)** [***Issue***]—The model for sales forecasting and distribution planning at Ellington will integrate existing and planned systems (OSB and MRP). Our significant background with OSB and our involvement with the MRP project will help incorporate the new sales forecasting and DRP model into the systems environment at Ellington [***Conclusion & Data***].

- **System Management Methodology** [***Issue***]—Our consultants have valuable experience employing the practical techniques embodied in our methodology, SMM. We can help guide the approach for completing each stage of the sales forecasting and DRP project [***Conclusion & Data***].

- **"Shoulder-to-Shoulder" Staffing Approach** [***Issue***]—Our approach to organization of this project is to be a day-to-day participant. Our "shoulder-to-shoulder" approach permits us to function as a catalyst to the project team. In addition, we will supplement project personnel in the completion of key tasks, where appropriate [***Conclusion & Data***].

- **Large-Scale Systems Development and Implementation Experience** [***Issue***]—We will draw upon our experience in evaluating, designing, and implementing large-scale business systems as we help the project team with each stage of the project. We will bring the practical experience with systems evaluation, design, and implementation that is key to success in highly integrated systems like sales forecasting and DRP [***Conclusion & Data***].

As a final point, we appreciate the opportunity to further demonstrate the contribution we can make to Ellington. We regard Ellington as a valuable client and hope we will have the opportunity to assist you with this project [***Conclusions***].

We trust this proposal conveys our enthusiasm for assisting you and Ellington Electronics with this important first stage of the project [***Assumption***]. If you have any questions, please call me at (406) 123-4567 [***Action Program***].

Very truly yours,

Attachment

A Persuasive Cover Letter for a Proposal

The next proposal is more successful in conveying the proposing firm's qualifications for the job. The conversational tone makes the document readable and credible, because it feels genuinely sincere. As noted in discussion of the previous example, Conclusions are only as persuasive as the Data that supports them. And in this proposal, the writer provides concrete examples to substantiate each of the Conclusions.

Presenting Dorsey & Dorsey's eight qualifications in two lists also makes it easier for the reader to absorb these details. Notice how the qualifications are divided into those that make the firm suited for this specific engagement, and those general attributes that account for the firm's success.

The next to last paragraph summarizes the usual sections of a proposal, and their order in the attachment. The attachment is not included here, since examples of the "One-Page Memo with Attachments" format can be found in Chapters 2 and 3.

Dear Ella:

I enjoyed meeting with you, Zoot, and Woody last Friday [**What Prompts Your Document Now**]. I believe Tommy and I have a better understanding of what you are attempting to accomplish in the Planning & Analysis area for First Dubuque Bank's Capital Markets Sector. We are delighted that you are considering using the resources of Dorsey & Dorsey for this executive recruiting assignment [**Importance of Subject**].

I believe First Dubuque should select our firm for this assignment [**Position**] based on three primary factors.

1. **We know First Dubuque**—We have been doing search work for the bank since 1999.
2. **We know the Sector Controller job**—Tommy and I successfully recruited Roy Eldridge for the CCI sector.
3. **We know the trading area**—Tommy and I are familiar with the character of the department and the personalities of the individuals with whom the successful candidate must deal. Not only will this be helpful in assessing candidates, but it will be invaluable in finding our way around most of the target firms [**Conclusions**].

In addition, there are further strengths that form the foundation of Dorsey & Dorsey and that account for our significant record of success and the resulting long-standing relationships we have enjoyed.

- *Our optimal size*—With 13 consultants and 18 people in Research and Support, we are big enough to have a wide spectrum of resources needed to maintain a quality data management system. At the same time, we are not so big that our partners and staff are anonymous voices to our network of sources.
- *Our pool of 4,000 quality executives at first-rate firms*—Over the past decade we have built and refined an intimate, medium-size, "live" network of approximately 4,000 successful, results-oriented managers and executives. Through personal contact as well as our newsletter *Finders/Keepers,* we stay in touch with each a minimum of three times annually.

- ***Critical tasks are not delegated downward***—We employ a top-heavy, team approach to searches. Our senior partners perform the critical tasks on their own searches, which differs from the practices of many of our competitors.
- ***The best Research Staff in executive recruiting***—Nonetheless, we operate on the assumption that research is too important to be left entirely to our researchers. The up-front effort, which focuses on contacting the best sources and through them compiling a rich source of quality candidates, is a joint effort between Research and the consulting staff.
- ***Access to a larger group of target firms***—Because of our smaller client list relative to other, larger search firms, we are not likely to be "closed out" of the best sources of your highest potential candidates [***Conclusions***].

Ella, in the attachment I have addressed the following topics: (1) our understanding of your situation and objectives; (2) the ideal candidate; (3) our proposed search process and the likely timing of results; (4) the dedicated staffing of this search; and (5) a financial proposal for the search [***Issues***].

As you can gather, Tommy and I would welcome this opportunity to work with you again in meeting your staffing needs [***Conclusion***]. I look forward to your response to this proposal. I will call you Friday to see if you need any further information [***Future Work***].

An Engineering Proposal

Having looked at more and less effective ways to use the *Spence & Company* structure to organize proposals, let's apply what we have learned to revising a few examples.

Following is a proposal submitted to a state agency for inspecting communication towers and reporting on their condition. The proposal makes the common mistake of summarizing the firm's services without making a case for why the agency should actually contract with this firm. Many professionals are unclear about how to sell their services in a professional manner. As a result, they adopt the "soft-sell" approach used in this proposal that basically tells the prospect, "Here's what we do. Let us know if you are interested." Not exactly a proactive way to go about business development in a competitive market.

In addition to the proposal's failure to sell the firm's services, it also requires the reader to review the entire document to understand the full range of services offered. This is also a common practice, and anyone who has been on the receiving end of such proposals knows how tedious it is to read all that detail. Imagine, in addition, how much more tedious it is to read a whole stack of such proposals and try to compare the various services offered.

Finally, the proposal is unnecessarily repetitive. Information under Tower Analysis is repeated in the following section on Reports.

Mr. Gavin Driscoll
Agreement Manager
KDOT HQ Facilities Office
7345 Grantsville Avenue SW
Downey, KS 66016

Subject: **Site Visit and Structural Analysis for typical KDOT towers.**

Dear Mr. Driscoll,

In response to your inquiry, RPD Engineering's Tower Engineering Group, is pleased to submit the following outline of the possible site visit and structural analysis services that RPD can provide for the typical Kansas Department of Transportation (KDOT) communication tower sites. RPD's structural and civil services are not limited to those identified below, however based on conversations with KDOT these are the services that can be expected to be performed for a typical KDOT tower site.

Structural Observation

Two RPD structural engineers will conduct a site visit and a full tower climb to observe the structural condition of the requested tower. Any observed structural deficiencies and recommended maintenance will be reported. Also, while on site the engineers will verify the location of all antennas and feed lines and any other information influencing the structural analysis of the tower. The site visit observations will be incorporated into any analyses performed after the visit. If documentation listing the tower's framing member sizes and dimensions is not available, RPD engineers will measure and document the tower's dimensions and member sizes.

Typically the Tower Engineers visiting the site are of the Technical Specialist and Design Engineer II level. Depending on the tasks needed to be performed, the height of the tower, size of the overall site, and the weather conditions, the engineers will require approximately two to four hours on site for a typical self-supporting tower. Completion of the tower climb and other tasks is subject to safe weather conditions.

Access to the tower sites will have to be coordinated with KDOT. Engineers are typically equipped with 4x4 SUVs to access tower sites. KDOT will be responsible for providing any special transportation, beyond SUVs, necessary for accessing the tower site unless specifically defined and negotiated in the tower's scope of work. The project scope is to include travel time and expenses for the two engineers from Kansas City, Kansas to the tower site.

Tower Analysis

The typical KDOT tower will be analyzed to determine conformance with the ANSI TIA/EIA-222-G standard with the following configurations:

- Existing tower configuration
- Tower construction to be based on the tower site visit, previous analysis reports, and tower drawings available to RPD Engineering and any additional information provided KDOT.
- Proposed tower configuration
- Analysis to include existing tower loading with any proposed antennas identified by KDOT.

When requested, other tower loading scenarios can be performed to help determine the optimal loading of the tower and the best course of action for KDOT.

Should the tower be found to be overstressed in any of the above conditions, RPD will identify overstressed members and comment on the feasibility of structural upgrades. Should KDOT choose to pursue the structural upgrades, RPD will be available to design the upgrades and provide construction drawings under a separately negotiated scope of work.

Report

A report will be prepared documenting the site visit observations and results of the structural analysis.

Should the tower be found to be overstressed in any of the above conditions, RPD will identify overstressed members and comment on the feasibility of structural upgrades. Should KDOT choose to pursue the structural upgrades, RPD will be available to design the upgrades and provide construction drawings under a separately negotiated scope of work.

Upgrade Design & Construction Drawings

If directed by KDOT, RPD will design any necessary tower upgrades and provide analysis to show conformance with the ANSI TIA/EIA-222-G standard with the following configurations:

- Upgraded tower with proposed loading configuration
- Analysis to be based off the previous existing tower loading with proposed antennas analysis model and will included the designed tower upgrades.

Construction drawings will be produced that illustrate the required structural upgrades for the addition of the proposed antennas. These drawings will be stamped and signed by a Kansas State Registered Engineer. The final set of drawings is intended to be used as the permit, bid, and construction set of drawings. Upgrade calculations will also be included as needed for any permit submittal. If requested, an updated analysis report will be produced that includes the tower's upgrade analysis model and an engineer's cost estimate for upgrade construction.

Construction Support Services

As negotiated with KDOT, RPD will provide construction support services during the construction process. Potential services to be provided include site visits for the pre-construction meeting, periodic construction milestones and final inspection, response to contractor's pre-construction meeting questions, and review of contractor's submittals. After the final inspection visit RPD will identify any punch list items and write a letter of acceptance to the owner at the completion of the project.

The attached billing rate schedule has been included for your information. The hours required for each tower will be negotiated separately when the specific scope of work to be performed is defined.

We look forward to working with you on the KDOT tower site observations and structural analyses.

Respectfully,

RPD Engineering

An Engineering Proposal—Revised

One certain way to ensure that a proposal gets the reader's attention is to make it easy for them the read and understand. If your proposal is one of five that a selection committee must review, imagine the advantage you have if everyone can look at the first page of your proposal and know in a glance the services you offer, the experience and qualifications you have, and the fee you propose. No ambiguity there. Compare that with having to flip through 10 or more pages of a proposal, trying to figure out what is being offered.

A primary purpose in presenting these rewrites is to illustrate the importance of structure in effective communication. In most cases, the information is the same in the revision as in the original. Only the order in which the information is presented has been changed.

In this case, however, the original proposal has no Position. The reader is not asked to do or believe anything in particular about RPD Engineering's communication tower services. The proposal is a merely informational account of RPD's services. And even then, there is no presentation of RPD's qualifying experience, nor any information about similar clients or comparable engagements.

So, to turn this proposal into a document that actually advocates for RPD's services, a Position has been invented: RPD Engineering's tower engineering services are the most comprehensive in the Mid-West. To make this a truly effective proposal, however, the presentation would require more work to explain why this is in fact the case.

Mr. Gavin Driscoll
Agreement Manager
KDOT HQ Facilities Office
7345 Grantsville Avenue SW
Downey, KS 66016

Subject: **Site Visits and Structural Analysis Services for KDOT Towers**

Dear Mr. Driscoll,

Thank you for the opportunity to submit the following outline of site visit and structural analysis services that RPD Engineering's Tower Engineering Group can provide for the Kansas Department of Transportation (KDOT) communication tower sites [**What Prompts Your Document Now**].

As part of our full range of structural and civil engineering services, RPD Engineering offers the most comprehensive tower engineering services in the Mid-West [**Position**]. Please notify me if any of your needs are not addressed by the following outline of services [**Action Program**]. In particular, our tower engineering services include [**Issues**]:

1. **Site Visit and Structural Observation**—Site visits are conducted by two RPD structural engineers, and include a full tower climb. A site visit for a typical self-supporting tower requires between two and four hours.
2. **Tower Analysis and Report**—A tower analysis is conducted to determine the conformance with the ANSI TIA/EIA-222-G standard and optimal tower loading, identify overstressed members, and recommend structural upgrades, all of which is documented in a formal report.
3. **Upgrade Design and Construction Drawings**—RPD is prepared to design structural upgrades that are needed and prepare construction drawings for use during the permit, bid, and construction phases of the project.
4. **Construction Support Services**—RPD offers complete construction support services, including site visits for the preconstruction meeting, construction milestone and final inspections, response to contractor's pre-construction questions, and review of contractor's submittals.

A complete description of the above services is included in the attachment, together with our schedule of professional fees. The scope of a site visit and structural analysis and the hours required to conduct the necessary services are determined and agreed upon separately for each tower before work is performed [**Essential Background**].

We look forward to working with you on the KDOT tower site observations and structural analyses. I will call you next week to answer any questions you may have and to discuss your specific needs for communication tower inspections [**Future Work**]. In the meantime, you can reach me by phone at (913) 427-8808 [**Action Program**].

Respectfully,

RPD Engineering
Attachments

Attachment—RPD Site Visit and Structural Analysis Services for KDOT Towers

1. Site Visit And Structural Observation

Two RPD structural engineers conduct a site visit and a full tower climb to observe the structural condition of the tower. Typically the Tower Engineers visiting the site are qualified Technical Specialists and Design Engineer Level II professionals.

A site visit normally requires between two and four hours for a typical self-supporting tower, depending on the tasks to be performed, the height of the tower, the overall size of the site, and the weather conditions. Completion of the tower climb and other tasks is subject to safe weather conditions.

Any structural deficiencies and recommended maintenance are documented. While on site the engineers also verify the location of all antennas, feed lines, and any other information that will affect the structural analysis of the tower. RPD engineers also measure and document the tower's dimensions and member sizes, if these are not available.

Access to the tower sites is coordinated with KDOT. Engineers typically access tower sites by 4x4 SUV, unless special transportation provided by KDOT is needed. The scope of each project includes travel time and expenses for the two engineers from Kansas City, Kansas to the tower site.

2. Tower Analysis & Report

Each KDOT tower is analyzed to determine conformance with the ANSI TIA/EIA-222-G standard with respect to:

- Existing tower configuration, based on the tower site visit, previous analysis reports and tower drawings, and any additional information provided by KDOT.
- Proposed tower configuration, based on existing tower loading with additional antennas proposed by KDOT.

The RPD tower analysis identifies overstressed members and recommends structural upgrades. When requested, other tower loading scenarios can be performed to determine optimal loading of the tower and the best course of action for KDOT.

A report is prepared documenting the site visit observations and results of the structural analysis.

3. Upgrade Design & Construction Drawings

If the tower is found to be overstressed and KDOT wants to pursue structural upgrades, RPD is available to design the upgrades and provide construction drawings under a scope of work separate from the site visit and tower analysis.

As part of the design of structural upgrades, RPD documents that the upgraded tower, the proposed loading configuration, and the antenna analysis model conform to the ANSI TIA/EIA-222-G standard.

A final set of construction drawings, stamped and signed by a Kansas State Registered Engineer, is prepared for use during permit, bid, and construction phases of the project.

Upgrade calculations needed for any permit submittals are also prepared. If requested, an updated analysis report is produced that includes the tower's upgrade analysis model and an engineer's cost estimate for the upgrade construction.

4. Construction Support Services

RPD is also available to provide construction support services for structural upgrades, including site visits for the preconstruction meeting, construction milestone inspections, a final inspection, response to contractor's pre-construction questions, and review of contractor's submittals.

After the final inspection and completion of the project, RPD identifies punch list items and writes a letter of acceptance.

An Architectural Proposal

The first step in many bidding processes is for competing firms to establish their qualifications to perform the requested services. Although the following architectural proposal was composed to fulfill that purpose, it goes about it in a manner that is anything but straight-forward. Consider the following shortcomings.

First of all, the paragraphs are too long. The reader has to practically fight their way through all the detail, sentence by sentence. Nowhere can I simply scan the document to get a gist of why I should consider this firm for the job.

Second, the proposal is painfully clichéd. "Michelson Daly Architecture is sincerely interested…" "Please enjoy reviewing this response to your RFQ…" We hope you "will invite our team to personally convey our capabilities, enthusiasm and commitment." The overstated enthusiasm comes across as unconvincing and, therefore, unprofessional.

Third, in the second paragraph beginning "Appleton itself is a growing community…," the proposal makes the common mistake of telling the reader information about their organization or project that they already know. In this case, Michael Friley, the recipient, will have to read all about the community of which he is the Chief of Police, including where it is located. If you need to include this kind of information to confirm details of a project's scope, do so in an attachment in a section labeled "Background" or "Project Scope."

All in all, the proposal is not organized to achieve a purpose, namely to systematically document Michelson Daly's qualifications as an architectural firm, in a way that will be convincing to the reader.

Mr. Michael D. Friley, Chief of Police
Facilities Project Manager
40 East Maple Street
Appleton, WI 54911

RE: Request for Statements of Qualifications for Police/Court/IS Facility and Library
      Facility

Dear Michael,

Michelson Daly Architecture is sincerely interested in developing a relationship with the community of Appleton as we assist you in your efforts to deliver both the Police/Court/IS Facility and the Library Facility. The planning that has occurred during the last six years and the recent successful bond measure show the level of perseverance and support for these new facilities. Our team experience in planning, and designing public facilities will support your need to define a campus environment for "Academy Square". You will note that we have supplemented the team that was utilized to develop the Department of Public Safety Standards and Training campus with the addition of Whitehead Architects as our Police Design Consultant. Dan Whitehead has extensive knowledge of the intricacies of Police Station Design and will effectively supplement our experience in programming, master planning, community engagement, design and construction within the Fox River Valley environment.

Appleton itself is a growing community with proximity to I-41, Lake Winnebago, Little Chute, and Kaukauna. It also shares services and adjacency with Green Bay, New

London, and Oshkosh. Upgraded and modern public facilities are essential to meet the demands of a vibrant developing city. Even though there is a heightened awareness for safety and security within public buildings, we are challenged to create facilities that are open, inviting and non-threatening. Security and safety features need to seamlessly integrate with public facilities without offending or imposing on the community they are designed to serve. Additionally, community members need to have access to the planning process to both solicit input and maintain transparency and open communication so that all community members have a stake in "their" facility.

Our approach to the planning and design process has been honed after over forty years of collaborative practice. Although it is imperative that the final project incorporate the needs and requirements of the facility occupants, a successful project must take into account and manifest the physical, historical and cultural factors of the community it is designed to serve. We will study the physical and environmental forces contingent upon the development of these two sites. Considerations such as access to I-41 from W College Avenue and adjacency to Highway 441 will be analyzed along with buffer requirements to adjacent residential neighborhoods and the railroad line to the west of the police facility site. Input will be solicited from the community in public forums designed to further the goals and requirements of the facility needs assessment. The needs assessment will be validated through workshops with the user groups and we will meet with local authorities to solicit input on public infrastructure, roads, zoning and building codes.

We also have experience in Construction Manager / General Contractor (CM/GC) project delivery methods and will participate in the selection of this most important team member. The Department of Public Safety Standards and Training Facility in Green Bay was delivered utilizing the CM/GC process and this project successfully completed ahead of schedule and budget. Our approach to this project will be developed in detail with you as we have an opportunity to work together to outline your project plan.

Please enjoy reviewing this response to your RFQ for both the Police/Court/IS Facility and the Library Facility. We look forward to your questions and comments and hope you find our qualifications deserve further consideration and will invite our team to personally convey our capabilities, enthusiasm and commitment. Thank you.

Sincerely,

An Architectural Proposal—Revised

The preceding proposal has been revised below to create a focused presentation of the architectural firm's professional qualifications, and to remove anything that might distract from this purpose.

False enthusiasm and earnestness have been edited out. Paragraphs have been kept to a maximum of four to five sentences to enable the reader to scan the document. The firm's qualifications are summarized in a bulleted list that the reader can also scan and then use as a guide to additional information in the attachment.

The document gradually steps the reader through the detail. If the reader does not get beyond the first page, we can be reasonably sure that he or she will have grasped the essential message about Michelson Daly Architecture's qualifications that the proposal is intended to convey.

Mr. Michael D. Friley, Chief of Police
Facilities Project Manager
40 East Maple Street
Appleton, WI 54911

Subject: Michelson Daly Qualifications for Police/Court/IS Facility and Library Facility

Dear Michael,

Thank you for the opportunity to submit for your consideration the qualifications of Michelson Daly Architecture to assist you and the community of Appleton in the design and construction of both the Police/Court/IS Facility and the Library Facility [*What Prompts Your Document Now*]. Our hope is that our qualifications will sufficiently win your confidence that our team will be invited to present our capabilities in person [*Assumption*].

Our approach to the planning and design of public buildings has been refined over forty years of practice. We believe, in particular, that our team experience in planning and designing public facilities will support your need to define a campus environment for "Academy Square" [*Position*].

Michelson Daly has particular strength in the following areas, which we see as critical to the success of both the Police/Court/IS Facility and the Library Facility [*Conclusion*]. These qualifications are discussed in more detail in the attachment.

- Involving the community in the project's design and approval
- Creating a design that complements the community's unique characteristics
- Managing the project using Construction Manager / General Contractor (CM/GC) project delivery methods
- Integrating the new facility with the surrounding transportation infrastructure
- Incorporating safety and security features into the design in an aesthetic manner

To enhance our many years of experience in the design and construction of public facilities, we have included Whitehead Architects as our Police Design Consultant for the team that developed the Department of Public Safety Standards and Training campus in Little Chute. Dan Whitehead has extensive knowledge of the professional requirements of Police Station Design and will add to our existing strengths in programming, master planning, community engagement, design, and construction in the Fox River Valley [*Conclusion*].

We look forward to your questions and comments, and hope you find that our qualifications for the Police/Court/IS Facility and the Library Facility deserve further consideration [*Action Program*].

Sincerely,

Attachments

Attachment: Michelson Daly—Statement of Qualifications for Police/Court/IS Facility and Library Facility

We at Michelson Daly see the following six considerations as areas of our competence and expertise that will be critical to the successful completion of both the City of Appleton Police/Court/IS Facility and the Library Facility:

- **Community participation in the project's design and approval**—Input will be solicited from the community in public forums designed to further the goals and requirements of the facility needs assessment. The needs assessment will be validated through workshops with the user groups. We will also meet with local authorities to solicit input on public infrastructure, roads, zoning, and building codes. In addition, community members will be invited to participate in the planning process in order to solicit their input, maintain transparency and open communication, and enable community members to develop a stake in the facility as their own.

- **Design that complements the community's unique characteristics**—Although the final building must address the needs of the facility's occupants, a project's design must also reflect the physical, historical, and cultural characteristics of the community it is designed to serve. To this end, we will study the physical and environmental factors that will affect the development of the two sites.

- **Extensive experience in Construction Manager / General Contractor (CM/GC) project delivery methods**—We will participate in the selection of this most important team member. The Department of Public Safety Standards and Training Facility in Green Bay was delivered utilizing the CM/GC process and was successfully completed ahead of schedule and budget.

- **Integration of the facility with the surrounding transportation infrastructure**—Considerations such as access to I-41 from W College Avenue and adjacency to Highway 441 will be analyzed, along with buffer requirements to adjacent residential neighborhoods and the railroad line to the west of the police facility site.

- **A balance of safety, security, and design**—Although there is a heightened awareness of the need for safety and security considerations in the design and construction of public buildings, we are also aware of the need to create facilities that are open, inviting and non-threatening. Security and safety features need to seamlessly integrate with public facilities without offending or imposing on the community they are designed to serve.

- **Expertise in Police Station Design**—We have added Whitehead Architects to the team as our Police Design Consultant. Whitehead Architects developed the Department of Public Safety Standards and Training campus in Green Bay. Dan Whitehead has extensive knowledge of the professional requirements of Police Station Design and will enhance our experience in programming, master planning, community engagement, design, and construction in the Fox River Valley.

A Fee Change Proposal

Uh-oh. Somebody messed up, the project is over budget. Somebody has to pay, and it ain't gonna be you.

Well, I guess you can call that a proposal. Or at least a proposal is one way to handle that kind of situation in a professional manner. The secret is to make them an offer they can't refuse…

In the following proposal, an engineer is writing to an architect to explain why the architect owes the engineer money for services not covered in their original scope of work. The problem, however, is not the money. The problem is really that the proposal is made with a sledgehammer when it needs to be done with a scalpel. Let's look more closely at the problem.

The engineer was probably anxious about asking the architect for more money. So, in an attempt to make an air-tight case in his or her favor, the engineer wrote a long document to make the case for the change in fees, giving the rationale for each change in a long paragraph of supporting evidence.

So, if you were the architect, what would you do? Skip all the detail and turn to the last page to see the final bill, right? But even then, the document gives no satisfaction—there is no final bill, just more detail.

The alternative is to plod through the whole document, paragraph by paragraph, reading all the detail. Go ahead—see if you have the patience.

Mr. Pat Savage
Quimby Marsh Architects
135 Atlantic Way Southwest
Savannah, GA 31406

Subject: New Recreation Center at Triple Creek Ranch
           Additional Structural Services for Redesign and Added Scope

Dear Pat:

It has been a pleasure working with you on the new facility at Triple Creek Ranch. I enjoy being a part of the Quimby Marsh team, and working with a team committed to such a high level of design.

ADDED SCOPE & FEES

As you and I have discussed, there have been several recent design revisions and scope additions that have led to considerable redesign by Atwood Engineering. These design revisions have also led to the construction drawings being issued in several packages, rather than the two agreed upon in our contract scope. Following is a brief description of each issue, and an approximate additional fee.

Athletic Shop Truss/Layout:

Currently, we are on at least the 3rd configuration of the Athletic Shop roof truss and vertical support system. At the end of the DD phase, we had a concept that was structurally sound. Just prior to issuing the Athletic Shop foundations for Construction, Quimby Marsh redesigned the roof truss configuration. Since that time, we have worked through 2 concepts with you, before reaching the current configuration. The impact to the structural design has been substantial. We have added and moved columns, changed basement wall and pier relationships, and added new foundation elements to pick up the additional structural members. We have redesigned areas of the foundations, basement walls, piers, concrete and wood columns, PT slabs, and roof members. And, we have modified drawings that were already complete for construction.

Approximate Structural Fee: $4,000

Fireplaces:

The stone masses and fireplaces in the Dining and Locker Wings have undergone two iterations since the beginning of the CD phase. While each iteration has not been a substantial redesign effort, the two together combined with necessary plan and foundation changes has caused us to spend additional effort.

Approximate Structural Fee: $2,000

Trellis between Athletic Shop and Locker Wings:

A wood trellis and walkway was added between the Athletic Shop and Locker wings since the beginning of the CD phase. This added scope item was not included in our original contract. Our work to design this element has included foundations, tall cantilever retaining and site walls, wood member and connection designs, and lateral analysis for the overall system.

Approximate Structural Fee: $2,000

Out-of-the-box engineering (wood columns):

The built up wood columns in the Athletic Shop Wing do not adhere to conventional wood detailing as prescribed in the NDS code. We have spent and are spending, significant engineering time to design built up columns that meet the intent of the code and its tested provisions while also providing the dramatic spaced appearance of the architecture. This is beyond simple solid wood column design, as we are looking at composite wood and steel interaction, and coming up with creative solutions to use the appropriate scale wood sizes. This engineering effort was not assumed in our original proposal to you. The concepts we settled on during the schematic and design development phases did not include this type of built up wood column configuration. Creative engineering is one of our strengths, and certainly something we plan on doing for Quimby Marsh. However, we already spent a significant effort in this regard on the roof trusses and piers in the Locker and Dining wings during the schematic and design development phase.

Approximate Structural Fee: $4,500

Multiple CD packages:

We are committed to helping Quimby Marsh and your clients meet construction deadlines. As you know, the contractor was scheduled to start construction in late 2007, just before the redesign efforts above were undertaken. To help keep the contractor moving, we have had to issue several for-construction packages, instead of the two outlined in our scope. To date, we have issued four different for-construction packages, including one for foundations, and one each for the Dining, Locker, and Athletic Shop wing first floor decks.

Currently, it appears we will be issuing at least one additional for-construction package, for the roofs and the remainder of work. These five for-construction packages are substantially more than the two included in our scope. As you know, issuing construction documents in multiple packages requires more effort than issuing them at the same time.

Approximate Structural Fee: $7,500

I understand many of these issues may not be owner driven, and as such may be difficult to approve additional fees for. If there is anything else we can do to aid you in your discussions with the owner, please let us know. We are committed to Quimby Marsh and the new Triple Creek Ranch facility, and look forward to its successful completion. If you have any questions please call me at (912) 433-5500.

Sincerely,

Design Principal

A Fee Change Proposal—Revised

When you need to communicate bad news, do it quickly and cleanly, rather than slowly and laboriously. Give your reader the bad news right up front, so at least they know the extent of the damages. Then summarize your case, and tell them where in the document they will find a complete presentation of the supporting evidence. In that way, there is no mystery about what has happened, and no surprises. Then the reader can read calmly through whatever details they need to understand and verify your account of what needs to be done.

Compare the revision on the following pages with the original. Which version would you prefer?

Mr. Pat Savage
Quimby Marsh Architects
135 Atlantic Way Southwest
Savannah, GA 31406

Subject: Recreation Center at Triple Creek Ranch
           Additional Structural Services for Redesign and Added Scope

Dear Pat:

As you and I have discussed, there have been several recent design revisions and scope additions to the Recreation Center project at Triple Creek Ranch that have required considerable redesign work by Atwood Engineering [**What Prompts Your Document Now and Importance of Subject**].

Whereas many of these issues have not been owner driven, making owner approval of the additional fees more difficult, they are services required by Quimby Marsh's design changes [**Position**]. If there is anything we can do to aid you in your discussions with the owner [**Future Work**], please let us know [**Action Program**]. The design revisions are listed below, and detailed in the attachment, with estimates of the additional structural engineering fees for each.

1. Redesign of roof truss configuration for Athletic Shop [**Conclusion**].
   Estimated Structural Fee: $4,000

2. Redesign of stone masses and fireplaces in the Dining and Locker Wings. [**Conclusion**] $2,000

3. Design of wood trellis and Walkway between Athletic Shop and Locker Wings [**Conclusion**]. $2,000

4. Redesign of wood columns in the Athletic Shop Wing to meet NDS code and achieve appropriate architectural appearance [**Conclusion**].
                                                                          $4,500

5. Preparation of three additional for-construction packages, beyond the two included in the original scope [**Conclusion**].
                                                                          $7,500

Total estimated for additional structural services: $20,000

We are committed to Quimby Marsh and the new Triple Creek Ranch facility, and look forward to its successful completion. If you have any questions please call me at (912) 433-5500 [*Action Program*].

Sincerely,

Design Principal

Attachment

Attachment—Additional Services and Fees

Following is a brief description of the additional structural services provided by Atwood Engineering for the Recreation Center project at Triple Creek Ranch, with an estimate of fees.

1. Athletic Shop Truss/Layout

Although the roof design was structurally sound at the end of the DD phase, Quimby Marsh redesigned the roof truss configuration just prior to issuing the Athletic Shop foundations for Construction [*Background of Issue*].

The impact to the structural design has been substantial [*Conclusion*]. Atwood Engineering has developed 2 concepts with you, and is currently on at least the 3rd configuration of the Athletic Shop roof truss and vertical support system.

We have added and moved columns, changed basement wall and pier relationships, and added new foundation elements to pick up the additional structural members.

We have redesigned areas of the foundations, basement walls, piers, concrete and wood columns, PT slabs, and roof members.

And, we have modified drawings that were already complete for construction [*Data*].

Estimated Structural Fee: $4,000

2. Fireplaces

The stone masses and fireplaces in the Dining and Locker Wings have undergone two design iterations since the beginning of the CD phase [*Background of Issue*]. While each iteration in itself has not required substantial redesign, the two together, combined with necessary plan and foundation changes, have required additional time and effort [*Conclusion*].

Estimated Structural Fee: $2,000

3. Trellis between Athletic Shop and Locker Wings

The wood trellis and Walkway added between the Athletic Shop and Locker wings since the beginning of the CD phase was not included in our original contract [*Conclusion*]. Our work to design this element has included foundations, tall cantilever retaining and site walls, wood member and connection designs, and lateral analysis for the overall system [*Data*].

Estimated Structural Fee: $2,000

4. Out-of-the-box engineering (wood columns)

We have spent, and are spending, significant engineering time redesigning the built-up wood columns in the Athletic Shop Wing to meet the NDS code for conventional wood detailing, while also conforming to the spaced appearance of the architecture [*Conclusion*].

This engineering effort was not included in the original project scope, nor during the schematic and design development phases. Although we are committed to providing the creative engineering solutions that we excel in, we have already provided this kind of additional effort on the redesign of the roof trusses and piers in the Locker and Dining wings during the schematic and design development phase [*Data*].

Estimated Structural Fee: $4,500

5. Multiple CD packages

Currently, it appears we will be issuing at least five for-construction packages, which is substantially more than the two included in our scope [*Conclusion*]. As you know, issuing construction documents in multiple packages requires more effort than issuing them at the same time [*Background of Issue*].

The contractor was scheduled to start construction in late 2007—just before the redesign efforts above were undertaken. To help keep the contractor on schedule, as is our commitment, Atwood Engineering has had to issue more than the two for-construction packages outlined in our scope. To date, these include four different packages—one each for foundations and for the Dining, Locker, and Athletic Shop wing first floor decks. It appears as well that we will be issuing at least one additional package for the roofs and the remainder of work [*Data*].

Estimated Structural Fee: $7,500

Total estimated for additional structural services: $20,000

5. Readable Reports

I OFTEN HEAR WORKSHOP PARTICIPANTS SAY, "WE SPEND HOURS compiling 20-, 30-, 40-page reports, but our clients never read them!" I think we can safely assume that this is also true of 5 to 10 page reports.

An effective report, therefore, is one that summarizes your findings on the first page. That way, your readers will not miss the most important information, even if they don't read the rest of your report.

The problem with many reports is that they follow the format for lab reports that most of us learned in school. The report begins with a brief statement of the "presenting problem," or the purpose of the study, followed by a description of the methods used to gather data and a presentation of the results of the investigation. Conclusions and Recommendations are only summarized on the last page or so.

Under the circumstances, many people develop strategies for reading these Mystery Stories. They look at the first few paragraphs to see what the report is about, skip to the end to review the Conclusions and Recommendations, and then decide if they need to review the detail for supporting evidence.

Save your readers from having to figure out what your report is about, why they should accept your Conclusions, and where the most important information is. Give them all this critical information in the Opening Statement. Tell them your Position, or what you want them to do or believe, provide a brief account of essential information they need to understand the solution or evaluation you are advocating, and summarize your primary Conclusions and Recommendations. Then explain how the details of your study and its results are organized in the Body of the report.

A well-crafted Opening Statement should summarize the entire contents of your report. In this way, you ensure that your readers won't miss important information if they don't read the entire document. And by telling them how the rest of the report is organized, they can read your report selectively, concentrating on the information that is most important to them.

The current chapter applies this approach to shorter reports. The following chapter, "Format for Long Reports," explains how to organize reports of 20 pages or more.

Let's begin with an example of an Opening Statement that serves as an Executive Summary.

An Executive Summary

Part of the problem many people have in writing reports is that they become so focused on the Data that they fail to see that they actually have a point of view. They present their findings as if they were merely informational accounts of pure data collection, produced through completely objective means, without human intervention. The reality is usually that their study has in fact led them to a set of Conclusions that the reader has hired them to identify so that a decision can be made about what to do next.

The purpose of an Opening Statement or Executive Summary is to present that point of view.

Although an Executive Summary is often written after the rest of the report has been assembled, the approach to business and technical writing explained in *Organizing Ideas* suggests that it may be more efficient to outline and write an Executive Summary before you write the rest of the report. That way, you can decide what information to include and the best way to organize it at the beginning of the writing process, rather than trying to decide those questions while you are writing the report.

Planning and writing the Executive Summary before writing the rest of the report requires first that you identify your Position. Identifying your Position enables you to identify what information you will need to include to prove or support the point of view you are advocating.

Following is the Executive Summary of a study to determine the necessity for seismic upgrades to a bridge. The original summary has the feel of an informational report. The Position and the Recommendations are buried in the fourth paragraph, after a quantity of unnecessary detail about the location and history of the bridge. As too often happens, critical information is not presented in a way that is easy for readers to understand.

Executive Summary

This project is part of California Department of Transportation's (CDOT) effort to improve the seismic performance of its existing bridges under the Seismic Retrofit Program. The purpose of this study is to evaluate the Pacific Highway Bridge under seismic loading. Seismic retrofit of the bridge superstructure was completed during the first phase of the project in 1998. This study will evaluate the effectiveness of a supplemental seismic retrofit of structural elements located between the top of the bridge foundation and the superstructure.

The Pacific Highway Bridge is a 3,335-foot long highway bridge with a 33-foot roadway width. The bridge is located along State Route 20 at milepost 33.5 and carries the eastbound traffic between Cedar City and Red River. The bridge is comprised of a nine span post tensioned concrete west approach, a five span steel plate girder main span, and a seven span post tensioned concrete east approach. Earlier superstructure retrofit work included the installation of longitudinal seismic restrainers along all intermediate expansion joints, and the installation of transverse restrainers at the piers where the approach spans meet the main steel span.

A multimode elastic analysis was performed using a site-specific response spectrum. The recommended site-specific response spectrum was developed for a seismic event having a ten percent probability of exceedance in 50 years. The analysis results showed that the bridge columns lack ductility due to poor reinforcement detailing in the plastic hinge region. Also, the bridge foundations are undersized and have inadequate shear and flexural strength. Also, the timber pile to footing connection lacks any tension capacity causing footing uplift at very low load demands.

Based on the analysis results and discussions between Simmons Engineering and CDOT Bridge and Structures Office, it was determined that seismic retrofit of the substructure of the Pacific Highway Bridge is cost prohibitive. Bridge foundation damage is anticipated to occur at loads much lower than the loads associated with plastic hinging of the columns. Therefore, any column retrofit scheme will not be effective unless it is accompanied by a comprehensive foundation retrofit strategy. Furthermore, the geotechnical analysis of the site showed that there is potential for soil liquefaction at soil layer elevations far below the existing timber pile tip elevations. Therefore, the bridge foundation retrofit strategy will also have to address the liquefaction potential for this site, which is also very costly.

The analysis results also show that retrofit of some superstructure elements is required. The steel plate girders bearing pins are deficient at Piers 11, 12, 13, and 14. Similar to the retrofit scheme performed earlier by CDOT at Piers 10 and 15, we recommend retrofitting the bearing pins by installing transverse restrainers on each side of each bearing. Also, the number of longitudinal seismic restrainers provided across the expansion joints at Piers 2 and 7 is inadequate. We recommend adding a minimum of one longitudinal seismic restrainer over Piers 2 and 7.

An Executive Summary—Revised

The following revision highlights the study's key Conclusions and Recommendations, leaving no ambiguity about the work that needs to be done on the bridge, and why.

Executive Summary

The purpose of the following study was to evaluate the Pacific Highway Bridge under seismic loading and the effectiveness of a seismic retrofit of structural elements located between the top of the bridge foundation and the bridge's superstructure [***What Prompts Your Document Now***].

The Pacific Highway Bridge is a 3,335-foot long highway bridge with a 33-foot roadway width. The bridge is located along State Route 45 at milepost 33.5 and carries the traffic between Cedar City and Red River. The bridge consists of a nine-span post tensioned concrete west approach, a five-span steel-plate girder main span, and a seven-span post tensioned concrete east approach [***Essential Background***].

Based on analysis of the study's results, Simmons Engineering and the California Department of Transportation (CDOT) Bridge and Structures Office determined that a seismic retrofit of the substructure of the Pacific Highway Bridge is cost prohibitive [***Position***] because [***Conclusions***]:

1. Bridge foundation damage is expected to occur at loads much lower than those associated with plastic hinging of the columns, making any column retrofit scheme ineffective unless it is accompanied by a comprehensive foundation retrofit strategy.
2. A foundation retrofit would also require a solution to the site's potential for liquefaction at soil layers far below the depth of the existing timber pile tips.

The study also showed that [***Conclusions***]:

1. Bridge columns lack durability due to poor reinforcement detailing in the plastic hinge region.
2. Bridge foundations are undersized and have inadequate shear and flexural strength.
3. The timber-pile-to-footing connection has no tension capacity, causing the footing to rise at very low load demands.

The study also identified the need to retrofit the following superstructure elements:

- Transverse restrainers need to be installed on each side of the steel-plate girder bearing pins at Piers 11, 12, 13, and 14, similar to the retrofit performed by CDOT in 1998 at Piers 10 and 15.
- A minimum of one longitudinal seismic restrainer needs to be added to Piers 2 and 7, where the number of restrainers provided across the expansion joints is inadequate [***Recommendations***].

A multimode elastic analysis was performed using a site-specific response spectrum [***Sources of Data***]. The spectrum was developed for a seismic event with a ten percent probability of being exceeded over a 50-year time span [***Assumptions & Limitations***].

The project is part of CDOT's Seismic Retrofit Program to improve the seismic performance of existing bridges. A seismic retrofit of the bridge superstructure was completed in 1998, during the first phase of the project. Earlier superstructure retrofits included installing longitudinal seismic restrainers along all intermediate expansion joints and transverse restrainers at the piers where the approach spans meet the main steel span [***Essential Background***].

An Engineering Report

The engineering report that follows starts off as it should by telling readers What Prompts the Document Now: "A general conditions review and Probable Maximum Loss (PML) study was completed for the Piedmont Building as outlined in the proposal letter dated September 19, 2008. The purpose of this letter is to inform you of our findings and present you with the PML value." Good enough.

But immediately thereafter the report ensures that the reader will have to dig, decipher, and translate to figure out what the study discovered, or even where to find that information.

Try scanning the topic sentence of each paragraph. Is there any indication in those sentences as to where the important information lies? Not even the bulleted list is of help. There are eleven points of no recognizable importance.

Finally, the letter has the audacity to conclude with the Assumption that "the information regarding the general structural assessment and the PML value presented in this letter provides you with the information you need to present to your lender." What assessment? What PML value? Where? No doubt, they are buried in the building somewhere.

Mr. Matt Norton
Norton Properties, Inc.
1020 W 6th Street, Suite 850
Cleveland, OH 44109

Subject: Piedmont Building
           Probable Maximum Loss Estimate

Dear Matt:

A general conditions review and Probable Maximum Loss (PML) study was completed for the Piedmont Building as outlined in the proposal letter dated September 19, 2008. The purpose of this letter is to inform you of our findings and present you with the PML value.

The Piedmont Building, which was originally constructed in 1906, is a four-story building located at the south end of Little Chute. The original gravity framing system was composed of masonry bearing walls, timber columns, and a timber floor system. The original lateral force resisting system consisted of masonry shear walls that did not have reinforcing steel.

The original masonry lateral force resisting system was retrofitted in 1995. The retrofit included strengthening the roof and floor diaphragms, improving the connectivity of the diaphragms to the masonry shear walls, and adding supplementary braced frames. The original masonry shear walls were used for lateral force resistance in the north-south direction of the building, and supplementary braced frames were added on the westernmost side of the building to add another line of seismic resistance in the north-south direction. Two lines of braced frames were added in the east-west direction above Level 1. Below Level 1, four reinforced concrete shear walls were added in the east-west direction and two were added in the north-south direction to form a complete load path to the foundation.

A general assessment of the structural system was completed in accordance with the national standard *Seismic Evaluation of Existing Buildings* (ASCE/SEI 31, 2003). Part of this assessment included a site visit that was completed on September 27, 2008. The site visit, the ASCE/SEI 31 review, and the structural drawing review indicated that, overall, the building is well tied together and should distribute the lateral load to the foundation. Some of the observations made during the site visit include:

- There are locations where the timber beams have deteriorated; some of the deteriorated beams were partially removed and reinforced.
- There are locations where the timber columns have deteriorated. Various locations showed enough deterioration that the beam bearing plate on top of the column had tilted. It is advisable to strengthen/replace the columns with significant deterioration. In general, the material deterioration in the building was minimal and the deterioration observed at these columns seemed to be an isolated occurrence.
- It appeared that the rooftop unreinforced masonry parapet on the southeast corner of the building had been damaged and replaced with concrete.
- There are numerous filing cabinets that lined the corridors that could, if they were to topple over, inhibit egress following an earthquake.
- In addition to the above listed general observations, the following list includes the items that influenced the reported PML value:
- The story strength of the members in the lateral force resisting system changes by more than the 20 percent from level-to-level.
- The story stiffness of the members in the lateral force resisting system changes by more than the 30 percent from level-to-level.
- The diaphragms do not have continuous crossties (framing members) from chord-to-chord.
- The shear stress in the masonry walls was slightly higher than the prescribed 30 psi.
- There was masonry and timber material deterioration.
- There were slender, unbraced/unreinforced masonry parapets.

The results from the general assessment and the computer software program ST-Risk, which is a software package developed to estimate the potential financial losses due to earthquakes for a building, were used to complete the PML assessment. The PML is defined as the monetary losses for the building equal to the percentage of the cost necessary to completely replace the building in today's dollars. For example, if the cost to replace a building were $1,000,000, a PML of 15 would mean that the probable damage that may occur from an earthquake equates to 15 percent of the replacement cost, which would be equal to $150,000 in damage. The PML is defined for an earthquake that would produce accelerations with a recurrence interval of 475 years (10 percent probability of exceedance in a 50-year period).

The PML for the Piedmont Building estimated from ST-Risk was 16. The replacement cost of the building was estimated from the cost estimating reference RSMeans (2005) as $12,503,000. This number is not intended to be equal to the market value of the building, only the estimated cost to replace it. With a PML of 16, the total estimated monetary loss for an earthquake with a recurrence interval of 475 years would be approximately $2,000,000 (0.16 x $12,503,000).

I trust the information regarding the general structural assessment and the PML value presented in this letter provides you with the information you need to present to your lender. Should you have any questions or need further information, please call me at (216) 274-6255.

Sincerely,

Structural Engineer

An Engineering Report—Revised

In the following rewrite, the same information contained in the original report has been reorganized into the Opening Statement structure explained in *Organizing Ideas*. Each paragraph presents a relevant topic, which is identified in each topic sentence. The most important information is included in the cover letter. If the reader needs or wants to know more about the study's findings, these are available in the attachment.

The result is a report that is both detailed and scannable. The reader has a choice about how much detail they want to read. If they stop reading before the end, they have a pretty good idea what is contained in the remainder of the report, and can be sure they have not missed essential information.

Mr. Matt Norton
Norton Properties, Inc.
1020 W 6th Street, Suite 850
Cleveland, OH 44109

Subject: Piedmont Building
           Probable Maximum Loss Estimate

Dear Matt:

The purpose of this letter is to inform you of Sunset Engineering's findings from a general conditions review and Probable Maximum Loss (PML) study completed for the Piedmont Building, as outlined in our proposal dated September 19, 2008 [**What Prompts Your Document Now**]. I trust that this letter provides you with the information about the building's general structural condition and PML value that you need to present to your lender [**Importance of Subject**].

Our assessment of the Piedmont Building's overall structural condition is that it is well tied together and should distribute the lateral load to the foundation. We also estimate a PML for the building of 16, meaning that the total estimated loss from an earthquake with a recurrence interval of 475 years would be approximately $2,000,000 (0.16 x $12,503,000) [**Position**].

Probable Maximum Loss is an estimate of potential financial loss from earthquake damage, defined as a percentage of the cost in today's dollars of replacing the building due to an earthquake with a recurrence interval of 475 years, and a 10 percent chance in a 50-year period of that probability being exceeded [**Definition of Terms**]. For example, if the cost to replace a building were $1,000,000, a PML of 15 would mean that the probable damage from an earthquake would be 15 percent of the replacement cost, or $150,000.

The determination of Probable Maximum Loss is based on a general structural assessment from a site visit, together with results generated by ST-Risk, a software program that estimates financial loss from earthquake damage to a building. Using RSMeans (2005) cost estimating as a reference, the Piedmont Building's replacement cost—not its market value—was estimated at $12,503,000 [*Sources of Data*]. With a PML of 16, the total estimated monetary loss for an earthquake with a recurrence interval of 475 years would be 0.16 x $12,503,000 or approximately $2,000,000 [*Conclusion*].

Our assessment is based on a site visit completed on September 27, 2008, a review completed in accordance with the national standard *Seismic Evaluation of Existing Buildings* (ASCE/SEI 31, 2003), and a review of the building's structural drawings [*Sources of Data*]. Details of the site visit and general structural review are included in the attachment.

If you have any questions or need further information, please call me at (216) 274-6255 [*Action Program*].

Sincerely,

Structural Engineer

Attachment

Attachment: Piedmont Building—Original Construction and 1995 Retrofit

Background

The Piedmont Building, which was originally constructed in 1906, is a four-story building located at the south end of Little Chute. The original gravity framing system was composed of masonry bearing walls, timber columns, and a timber floor system. The original lateral force resisting system consisted of masonry shear walls that did not have reinforcing steel.

The original masonry lateral force resisting system was retrofitted in 1995. The retrofit included strengthening the roof and floor diaphragms, improving the connectivity of the diaphragms to the masonry shear walls, and adding supplementary braced frames.

The original masonry shear walls were used for lateral force resistance in the north-south direction of the building, and supplementary braced frames were added on the westernmost side of the building to add another line of seismic resistance in the north-south direction.

Two lines of braced frames were added in the east-west direction above Level 1. Below Level 1, four reinforced concrete shear walls were added in the east-west direction and two were added in the north-south direction to form a complete load path to the foundation [*Essential Background*].

General Structural Assessment

A general assessment of the structural system was completed in accordance with the national standard *Seismic Evaluation of Existing Buildings* (ASCE/SEI 31, 2003). Part of this assessment included a site visit that was completed on September 27, 2008. The site visit, the ASCE/SEI 31 review, and the structural drawing review indicated that, overall, the building is well tied together and should distribute the lateral load to the foundation [*Sources of Data*].

Some of the observations made during the site visit include [*Data*]:

- Material deterioration in the building was generally minimal.
- Timber columns with significant deterioration should be strengthened or replaced. Although deterioration was generally an isolated occurrence, some columns had deteriorated to the extent that beam bearing plates on top of columns had tilted.
- Timber beams have deteriorated in some locations, some of which were partially removed or reinforced.
- The unreinforced masonry parapet on the southeast corner of the rooftop appears to have been damaged and replaced with concrete.
- Numerous filing cabinets lined the corridors that could prevent easy exit if they fell over during an earthquake.

Findings that Influenced the Probable Maximum Loss (PML) Evaluation

In addition to the general observations above, following are items that influenced the reported PML value:

- The story strength of the members in the lateral force resisting system changes by more than the 20% from level-to-level.
- The story stiffness of the members in the lateral force resisting system changes by more than the 30% from level-to-level.
- The diaphragms do not have continuous crossties, or framing members, from chord-to-chord.
- The shear stress in the masonry walls was slightly higher than the prescribed 30 psi.
- There was masonry and timber material deterioration.
- There were slender, unbraced or unreinforced masonry parapets.

An Environmental Consulting Report

People who are technically trained are often so focused on their Data that they forget that their purpose in writing is primarily to report the Conclusions and Recommendations that they have derived from their Data.

The following environmental consulting report illustrates this distinction. Someone needs the information in the report to decide what kind of sand and gravel to put in a trench. It is really that simple. As you read the report, however, consider how much time you spend just figuring out what the report is about and finding the information that will help someone make a decision. If you get impatient during your search, turn to the revised report that follows.

Introduction

This report, Grain Size Analysis for Recovery Trench Backfill, provides the rationale for the assigned parameters of the recovery trench backfill. These parameters are based on grain size distributions of native sediments along the hydraulic control and containment (HCC) boundary and of possible fill materials, and on the conditions for filter and drain design in Cedergren (1989). Various mixtures of fills were analyzed by averaging the grain size distributions from multiple materials. A similar analysis will be performed on other aspects of the HCC system, such as GAC and organoclay permeable reactive barriers.

Sample locations, sampling methods, laboratory methods, and filter and drain design parameters are summarized in Section 2 of this report. Section 3 presents and summarizes the findings of the analysis, and Section 4 presents a short discussion of the results.

1.0   Methods

2.1   Native Sediments

Three test pits were dug on 8/16/07 along the HCC alignment; see Figure 4-1 for test pit locations. HCC-TP1 was sampled at 12' below ground surface (bgs), HCC-TP2 from 12-14' bgs, and HCC-TP3 from 11-13' bgs (see Boring Logs in Section 5.0). These depths are located in the smear zone and the elevation of greatest Bunker-C contamination. Samples were analyzed for grain size distribution by Scientific Analysis, Incorporated (SAI) according to ASTM D422. HCC-TP1 12' was run in duplicate and HCC TP2 12-14' was run in quadruplicate.

2.2   Fill Materials

Five different fill materials from Morrison, Inc. gravel pits in proximity to the Site were analyzed: 2" screened pit run, shoulder ballast, gravel borrow, round rock, and sand. Grain size distribution for these materials was obtained from Morrison (see Section 5.0). The 2" screened pit run was analyzed by both Scientific Analysis, Inc. (SAI) and by Morrison Inc. Organoclay grain size distributions were obtained by the manufacturer, SEDCO Technologies. Grain size distributions for mixtures were calculated by averaging the grain size distributions of the constituents. Grain size distributions below 1" were calculated by dividing the percent for each fraction by the percent that passed below 1" for each distribution. The sieve sizes used for grain size distribution analysis from Morrison varied from fill to fill. Missing data points were interpolated assuming a linear relationship between percent passing and grain size, which are marked in bold on Table F3-1.

2.3   Filter and Drain Design Parameters

Cedergren (1989) outlines the grain size distribution constraints on drains (such as recovery trenches) adjacent to native sediments. These constraints are expressed in the percent sizes for each grain size distribution. For example, 85% grain size is the size at which 85% of the distribution falls below that grain size, and is expressed as D_{85}. The three constraints used for this analysis are:

Constraint #1)	$D_{15\,fill} > 5*D_{15\,native}$	
Constraint #2)	$D_{15\,fill} < 5*D_{85\,native}$	
Constraint #3)	$D_{50\,fill} < 25*D_{50\,native}$	(pp. 154-156)

The large grain sizes of the native sediment at this site result in the first constraint being most difficult to achieve. Importantly, for native sediments with large grain sizes, this analysis is performed only on the fraction of sediment finer than the 1 inch sieve (p. 157). A final parameter outlined is that the grain size distribution curve of the fill should be similar in shape (parallel) to the distribution curve of the native sediments (p. 156).

2.0   Results

Table F3-1 shows grain size distributions for native sediments and for fill materials, including corrections for grain sizes <1". Figures F3-1 and F3-2 show the grain size distribution curves for native sediment with and without accounting for grain sizes above 1", respectively. From these distributions, percent grain size for 85%, 50% and 15% passing were estimated for the average distributions for each test pit, and for the average of all samples analyzed (see Table F3-2). The data show coarse, heterogeneous sediments with percent passing varying up to 10% from sample to sample, and percent passing varying over 20% from test pit to test pit. In keeping with coarse sediments, the D_{15}, D_{50} and D_{85} values increased by 3 to 19 times when grain sizes above 1" were included for analysis. $D_{15\,avg} = 850$ μm for the full sieve analysis, and $D_{15\,avg,} = 250$ μm for the fraction < 1".

The constraints on the trench fill material were calculated using the average grain size distribution curve for all samples analyzed (see Table F3-3). The primary constraints for trench fill material are that $D_{15fill} > 1250$ μm, and $D_{50fill} < 60,000$ μm for trench fill grain sizes <1".

To find appropriate fill mixtures, a weighted average was used to test the grain size distributions for various fill ratios. Four mixes that fulfill the D_{15} and D_{50} criteria for grain sizes <1" are shown in Table F3-4, and graphed next to the average native fill curve in Figure F3-3. These mixtures are: mix 1—25% 2" pit run and 75% round rock; mix 2—15% sand and 85% round rock; mix 3—80% shoulder ballast and 20% 2" pit run; and mix 4—85% shoulder ballast and 15% gravel borrow. As a validity measure, these mixtures are graphed for the full range of grain sizes in Figure F3-4.

3.0   Discussion

The purpose of this analysis is to ensure that the recovery trench fill is coarse enough to provide sufficient hydraulic conductivity to drain the adjacent groundwater, and to ensure that the recovery trench is fine enough to prevent the erosion of smaller particles into the trench, in order to maintain the conductivity and integrity of the trench. Because of the coarse native sediment along the HCC alignment, producing a fill material that is very coarse and still has a natural grain size distribution curve is the major objective of this analysis. Thus, Constraint #1, which specifies that the D_{15} of the fill material is 1250 μm or more, or 5 times the average native D_{15}, is the most restrictive constraint. Given that the constraints listed in Cedergren (1989) are 4-5 times $D_{15native}$, this is slightly conservative.

It is difficult to achieve a parallel grain distribution curve for fill materials and native sediments (see Figures F3-3 and F3-4). For example, most of the round rock material is sized from ¾" to 1¼", creating a grain size distribution curve that does not match the natural sediment. Fills with more natural distribution curves, such as 2" screened pit run, contain too much fine material to make up a large proportion of the fill mixture. Of the four fill mixtures listed, mix 3 and mix 4 have the most natural grain size distribution curves.

Finally, the full grain size distribution curve is provided (Figure F3-4) as a validity measure for this analysis. The four fill mixes presented fulfill the constraints for both full grain distributions and <1", showing that they are adequate choices for trench backfill material.

An Environmental Consulting Report—Revised

The following revision presents the information the client needs in less than a page, and then provides a brief explanation of the information contained in the rest of the report.

The language is still a little more technical than is probably necessary, especially if the audience is not technically trained. Correcting that shortcoming, however, would require a lot of wordsmithing by someone with the skills to translate it into plain English. All of which would probably require considerable time and effort.

As it is, even non-technical people can, for the most part, understand what the report is about. So we will leave the language alone. The take-away here is that just changing the order in which the information is presented makes the report much more understandable.

Grain Size Analysis for Recovery Trench Backfill

1.0   Introduction

This report provides the rationale for the assigned parameters of the recovery trench backfill. The parameters are based on grain size distributions of native sediments along the hydraulic control and containment (HCC) boundary and of possible fill materials, and on the conditions for filter and drain design in Cedergren (1989) [**What Prompts Your Document Now**].

The purpose of this analysis is to ensure that the recovery trench fill is coarse enough to provide sufficient hydraulic conductivity to drain the adjacent groundwater, and to ensure that the recovery trench is fine enough to prevent the erosion of smaller particles into the trench, in order to maintain the conductivity and integrity of the trench [*Essential Background*].

Because of the coarse native sediment along the HCC alignment, producing a fill material that is very coarse and still has a natural grain size distribution curve is the major objective of this analysis [*Assumption*].

The four fill mixes presented fulfill the constraints for both full grain distributions and <1", showing that they are adequate choices for trench backfill material. Of the four fill mixtures listed, mix 3 and mix 4 have the most natural grain size distribution curves [*Position*].

Various mixtures of fills were analyzed by averaging the grain size distributions from multiple materials [*Sources of Data*]. A similar analysis will be performed on other aspects of the HCC, such as GAC and organoclay permeable reactive barriers [*Future Work*].

Section 2 of this report presents a short discussion of the results. Section 3 summarizes the grain size distribution constraints on drains, such as recovery trenches, adjacent to native sediments as determined by Cedergren (1989). Section 4 presents and summarizes the findings of the analysis. Section 5 summarizes sample locations, sampling methods, and laboratory methods. Boring Logs can be found in Section 6 [*Issues and Conclusions*].

2.0   Achieving a Parallel Grain Distribution Curve

It is difficult to achieve a parallel grain distribution curve for fill materials and native sediments (see Figures F3-3 and F3-4). For example, most of the round rock material is sized from ¾" to 1¼", creating a grain size distribution curve that does not match the natural sediment.

Fills with more natural distribution curves, such as 2" screened pit run, contain too much fine material to make up a large proportion of the fill mixture. Of the four fill mixtures listed, mix 3 and mix 4 have the most natural grain size distribution curves.

Finally, the full grain size distribution curve is provided (Figure F3-4) as a validity measure for this analysis. The four fill mixes presented fulfill the constraints for both full grain distributions and <1", showing that they are adequate choices for trench backfill material.

3.0   Filter and Drain Design Parameters

Cedergren (1989) outlines the grain size distribution constraints on drains (such as recovery trenches) adjacent to native sediments. These constraints are expressed in the percent sizes for each grain size distribution.

For example 85% grain size is the size at which 85% of the distribution falls below that grain size, and is expressed as D_{85}. The three constraints used for this analysis are:

Constraint 1	$D_{15\,fill} > 5*D_{15\,native}$	
Constraint 2	$D_{15\,fill} < 5*D_{85\,native}$	
Constraint 3	$D_{50\,fill} < 25*D_{50\,native}$	(pp. 154-156)

The large grain sizes of the native sediment at this site result in the first constraint being most difficult to achieve. Importantly, for native sediments with large grain sizes, this analysis is performed only on the fraction of sediment finer than the 1 inch sieve (p. 157).

A final parameter outlined is that the grain size distribution curve of the fill should be similar in shape (parallel) to the distribution curve of the native sediments (p. 156).

4.0   Results

To find appropriate fill mixtures, a weighted average was used to test the grain size distributions for various fill ratios. Four mixes that fulfill the D_{15} and D_{50} criteria for grain sizes <1" are shown in Table F3-4, and graphed next to the average native fill curve in Figure F3-3. These mixtures are:

- Mix 1   25% 2" pit run and 75% round rock
- Mix 2   15% sand and 85% round rock
- Mix 3   80% shoulder ballast and 20% 2" pit run
- Mix 4   85% shoulder ballast and 15% gravel borrow

As a validity measure, these mixtures are graphed for the full range of grain sizes in Figure F3-4.

As shown in Table F3-3, the constraints on the trench fill material were calculated using the average grain size distribution curve for all samples analyzed. The primary constraints for trench fill material are that $D_{15fill} > 1250$ μm, and $D_{50fill} < 60,000$ μm for trench fill grain sizes <1".

Table F3-1 shows grain size distributions for native sediments and for fill materials, including corrections for grain sizes <1".

Figures F3-1 and F3-2 show the grain size distribution curves for native sediment with and without accounting for grain sizes above 1", respectively. From these distributions, percent grain size for 85%, 50%, and 15% passing were estimated for the average distributions for each test pit, and for the average of all samples analyzed (see Table F3-2).

The data show coarse, heterogeneous sediments with percent passing varying up to 10% from sample to sample, and percent passing varying over 20% from test pit to test pit.

In keeping with coarse sediments, the D_{15}, D_{50}, and D_{85} values increased by 3 to 19 times when grain sizes above 1" were included for analysis. $D_{15\ avg} = 850$ μm for the full sieve analysis, and $D_{15\ avg,} = 250$ μm for the fraction < 1".

5.0   Methods

5.1   Native Sediments

Three test pits were dug on 8/16/07 along the HCC alignment; see Figure 4-1 for test pit locations. HCC-TP1 was sampled at 12' below ground surface (bgs), HCC-TP2 from 12-14' bgs, and HCC-TP3 from 11-13' bgs (see Boring Logs in Section 6.0). These depths are located in the smear zone and the elevation of greatest Bunker-C contamination.

Samples were analyzed for grain size distribution by Scientific Analysis, Incorporated (SAI) according to ASTM D422. HCC-TP1 12' was run in duplicate and HCC TP2 12-14' was run in quadruplicate.

5.2   Fill Materials

Five different fill materials from Morrison, Inc. gravel pits in proximity to the Site were analyzed:

- 2" screened pit run
- shoulder ballast
- gravel borrow
- round rock
- sand

Grain size distribution for these materials was obtained from Morrison (see Section 5.0). The 2" screened pit run was analyzed by both Scientific Analysis, Inc. (SAI) and by Morrison Inc.

Organoclay grain size distributions were obtained by the manufacturer, SEDCO Technologies.

Grain size distributions for mixtures were calculated by averaging the grain size distributions of the constituents. Grain size distributions below 1" were calculated by dividing the percent for each fraction by the percent that passed below 1" for each distribution. The sieve sizes used for grain size distribution analysis from Morrison varied from fill to fill.

Missing data points were interpolated assuming a linear relationship between percent passing and grain size, which are marked in bold on Table F3-1.

6. Format for Long Reports

FOR REPORTS OF MORE THAN TEN PAGES, A ONE-PAGE OPENING Statement may not be enough to summarize your Position and your major Conclusions and Recommendations. Although the elements of a 30- or 40-page report are the same as those in shorter reports, you may need to modify the structure a bit. Because the sections of a long report are expanded accounts of the elements in the Opening Statement, these elements are often placed in separate sections with headings such as *Introduction* or *Summary*.

In the example that follows, you will see that the first page is a cover letter containing the Opening Statement. This sequence is appropriate when the cover letter is bound into the report. In those instances in which it is not, the Executive Summary follows a short letter of transmittal. This cover letter begins by identifying the attached report, because the first question readers ask is, "What is this attachment?"

As usual, the Position appears as the topic sentence of the second paragraph. It is followed by the two Conclusions of the report that contribute most to proving the Position.

Finally, we see the two "next steps" in the Action Program—an Intermediate Feasibility Study and an Underground Evaluation Program. Because these constitute the project work for the coming years, they receive further explanation in the last two paragraphs of the cover letter.

Thereafter, we see the title page and Table of Contents that are standard in documents of more than ten pages.

The Introduction orients the readers by providing Essential Background, Definition of Terms, Sources of Data, and Assumptions & Limitations. We see the same information in shorter documents. However, in the report format these elements appear in a specific section, usually titled *Introduction,* because of the amount of information that may be required for each element.

After the example of the long report on the pages that follow, you will see a discussion of the Summary, the structure of the Body, and the use of a bibliography to identify additional sources of Data.

Ajax Minerals Company
P.O. Box 8910
Houston, Texas 77001

August 22, 2009
Santa Rena Project:
Preliminary Feasibility Study —
Prospects Favorable

Mr. Jabbo Smith
Ajax Minerals Company
P.O. Box 8910
Houston, Texas 77001

Dear Mr. Smith:

The attached report completes the preliminary study of the Santa Rena Project. It summarizes the highlights of the extensive financial and technical data obtained about the project from July 2008 to June 2009 [***Significance to the Readers, telling what is attached***].

The results of the Preliminary Feasibility Study confirm the initial estimates of extensive mineralization at the project site, indicating that the project is a worthwhile mining opportunity for Ajax Minerals Company [***Position***]. This assessment is supported by two factors: first, our projections of a Discounted Cash Flow Rate of Return as high as 19.7 percent, and second, our estimate that the mine will produce 7.5 million tons of material containing 1.72 percent copper and 2.53 percent zinc with 1.68 ounces of silver per ton [***Conclusions***].

Further research is required to refine project data to the level of confidence necessary to make a decision to develop the site. Therefore, the project team recommends that management approve the Intermediate Feasibility Study and an Underground Evaluation Program [***Action Program***].

The Intermediate Feasibility Study will further evaluate project economics based on alternative methods of development and ore treatment. The most viable method will be thoroughly investigated in the Final Feasibility Study. Additional work is also required on geology, reserves, water management, mine planning, ore tolling, mill process development, socio-economics, manpower, and marketing. This phase will begin immediately and finish at the end of 2010.

The Underground Evaluation Program will be conducted in the basal zone and will assess mineralization, determine hydrologic character and mining parameters, and collect a bulk sample for pilot plant testing. The program will begin in mid-2010 and finish at the end of 2011.

Very truly yours,

Project Manager

Attachment

Ajax Propriety
Report No. 25

Santa Rena Project

Grants County, New Mexico

Preliminary Feasibility Report

June 2009

Ajax Minerals Company
Mine Evaluation & Development Group

Table of Contents

Introduction

Ajax Minerals Company has conducted mineral exploration and pre-development activities at the 6,211-acre Santa Rena Project site in Monga National Forest in New Mexico since 2002. The discovery of mineralization at Santa Rena results from a zoned district study conducted by Ajax Minerals Exploration in the spring of 2005. Santa Rena was selected from 12 original sites as having the highest potential for a major copper deposit [*Background*].

Detailed work began in the spring of 2006 with a general survey of the area, geological mapping, land acquisition, additional geochemical sampling, and photogeology. The prospective site was submitted to management in the July 2007 budget and was approved for drilling. The first diamond drill hole revealed significant mineralization in the area, and additional holes outlined the extent of the mineralization presently referred to as the Santa Rena Project [*Background*].

This Preliminary Feasibility Report documents, in summary form, the results of evaluation work conducted during a study that began in July 2008 and extended until June 1, 2009. The purposes of the report are to:

- Document the major conclusions of this preliminary phase of evaluations, with particular emphasis on the presentation of financial analyses of the mining potential.
- Recommend further work required to more accurately evaluate the potential of the Santa Rena Project.

This report considers one means of developing and scheduling the exploitation of the Santa Rena deposit. The current conclusions will be further refined during the Intermediate and Final Feasibility Studies. This future work will improve the accuracy of current project economics, scope, and scheduling. The probable error of present capital and operating cost estimates is plus or minus 25 percent [*Assumptions & Limitations*].

This report presents only the most important conclusions and recommendations of the Preliminary Study. It is designed to be a decision-making tool for senior management. Therefore, it does not cover the full extent of the information compiled by the project team during the study.

However, a supplemental volume, containing the reports of the 18 work areas of the project, provides further data and is available upon request. A listing of the contents of this supplementary volume and other materials used or produced during the study is presented in the Bibliography at the end of this report [*Assumptions & Limitations*].

Summary

The results of five years of work by the Santa Rena Project team on the Preliminary Feasibility Study have confirmed our earlier estimates of significant mineralization at the project site and indicate that the project is a worthwhile mining opportunity for Ajax Minerals Company [*Position*].

A conclusive evaluation, however, requires further research. Consequently, the project team recommends that management approve the Intermediate Phase of the Feasibility Study and initiation of an Underground Evaluation Program [*Action Program*].

Projections of Mine Production

The mining operations at the Santa Rena site, as currently envisioned, will produce 2,500 tons of ore per day, five days a week, 250 days a year, or a total of 650,000 tons of material annually. The mine will operate for the ten-year period of 2013 – 2023 based on total estimated recoverable reserves of 7.5 million tons. Total employment for the mine and milling facility at full production is estimated at 245 [*Background*].

This study has assumed construction of a metallurgical processing facility at the project site to support the mining and concentrating operation. The project team has also examined the alternative of tolling the ore to an existing mill. However, tolling for the life of the project is prohibitive due to cost and inconvenience [*Assumptions & Limitations*].

Conclusions

The four primary findings of the study that support the assessment of the project as a major opportunity follow.

- The economics of the proposed mine and milling operation are favorable. One economic analysis for mining and milling the metals shows a Discounted Cash Flow Rate of Return of 19.7 percent—6.7 percentage points above the hurdle rate.
- Estimates of the mineral reserves currently place the total recoverable material at 7.5 million tons containing 1.72 percent copper and 2.53 percent zinc with 1.68 ounces of silver and 0.00 19 ounces of gold per ton.
- The feasibility of the project may depend on hydrologic conditions in the project area. This aspect of the project raises two concerns. First, there is some question about whether an adequate water supply exists in the area to process the material in the milling operation. Second, the groundwater, of which very little is currently known, might affect mining operations through flooding.
- The environmental issues associated with the project are sensitive, but compliance appears possible. Also, these issues will not seriously affect project economics [*Conclusions*].

Recommendations

The most important recommendations of the project call for approval of the Intermediate Feasibility Study and the initiation of an Underground Evaluation Program (UEP). Their intent and scope are outlined very briefly below:

- **Intermediate Feasibility Study**—The most critical work will be the hydrologic testing to determine the impact and availability of water at the project site. In addition, this phase will complete the environmental baseline work and continue to monitor environmental data.
- **Other studies during the Intermediate Phase** include work in the areas of socio-economic impact, geo-technical considerations, mining, energy, geology, ore processing, and contracting. This phase will extend approximately one and a half years and be completed at the end of 2011. Cost of the phase will be $2.9 million. This compares with $7.8 million spent on the Santa Rena Project to date [*Action Program*].
- **Underground Evaluation Program**—The project team has determined that the UEP represents the best means of evaluating the economic and technical viability of mining at Santa Rena. In this program, several steps will be taken to identify design parameters and determine operating conditions. First, sinking a nine-foot diameter vertical shaft will expose the overlying rock strata for geologic, rock mechanics, and hydrologic study.

Thereafter, the shaft will be extended to a depth of 1,250 feet to permit rock mechanics testing and operating design studies. Water inflows will be measured and mine drainage systems developed. Finally, a bulk sample will be obtained for metallurgical testing. The estimated cost of the UEP is $10,867,000, excluding contingency. It will begin in June 2010 and conclude at the end of 2011 (see Figure 1, Design and Production Schedule) [*Action Program*].

The remainder of this report provides additional detail for each of the four conclusions and the two recommendations in the same order as they are summarized above.

The Summary represents an expanded account of the information that appeared in the cover letter, consistent with the notion that the further the readers venture into the report, the more detail they receive. The Summary opens with the Position and Action Program. Then there is a brief account of Background, spelling out such details about the proposed mine as how much ore it will produce per day, how much it will produce over the course of the mine's operation, and total employment. We also see Assumptions & Limitations about the operation of a processing plant to support the mining effort.

The first two Conclusions at the bottom of the first page of the Summary appeared in the cover letter but here they receive a slightly expanded treatment.

The last two Conclusions on hydrologic and environmental concerns have not been discussed in the cover letter and here receive first mention. Then we see the two Recommendations considered in greater detail. Finally, a sentence of transition closes this section: "The remainder of this report provides additional detail for each of the four conclusions and the two recommendations in the same order as they are summarized above."

If you return to the Table of Contents, you will see that in the Body of the report each Conclusion and each Recommendation are substantiated with Data in several pages of text and in four tables and a figure.

With this structure, readers who are interested in project economics can read the cover letter, the Introduction, and Summary and then turn to page 5 of the report for the Data in text form and also look at the tables on pages 7, 8, and 9. The readers can skip aspects of the report that are not a concern and focus on those they need to know about.

Finally, the Table of Contents shows that at the end of the Body, on page 22, the report presents a Bibliography. This section directs the readers who want further Data on any of the Conclusions or Recommendations to supplemental sources, including a 400-page volume that contains the reports on the 18 work areas studied during the project. These materials, as noted at the bottom of the Introduction, are available upon request. If the readers need more information on project economics, the Bibliography tells them where to find such Data in the 400-page report.

7. Status Reports, Minutes, and Trip Reports

STATUS REPORTS, MINUTES OF MEETINGS, TRIP REPORTS, SITE VISITS, and call reports are among the most common types of standard business documents. Virtually everyone in business is responsible for writing one or more of these management reports on a regular basis.

All these documents serve a similar purpose. They evaluate.

The weekly, monthly, or quarterly report assesses the performance of a business unit, function, or activity. Minutes of meetings report on what has been accomplished at a meeting. Trip reports, site visits, and the call reports of salespeople relate the value of a trip or visit to a location or business.

Typically, however, these reports consist primarily of lists of activities, events, or observations, with little or no evaluation or commentary. Readers, and especially managers, are left to draw their own Conclusions about what the activities, events, or observations mean.

In other words, we tend to make the same mistakes when writing status reports, minutes of meetings, and trip reports that we make in all other types of business correspondence:

1. We fail to begin with an overview that presents our assessment and a list of the results or key points that we will discuss, and

2. We present our information in chronological order—the order in which the events occurred or we did the work.

These forms of reporting should all have the same structure as every other type of business communication. They all require the logical presentation of a Position, Conclusions, and Recommendations, as follows.

- Your **Position** is your assessment of the situation or activity that tells your readers to believe something.

- Your **Conclusions** are the key points or highlights of a meeting, trip, or reporting period.

- Your **Recommendations** are the action items you and your readers must take to capitalize on the results of the meeting, trip, or activity.

When composing status reports, minutes of meetings, and trip reports, follow the format presented on the *Worksheet for Organizing Ideas*. Start with an account of what prompts the correspondence—a meeting, trip, or end of the month. Then provide the Position—your evaluation of the month or your assessment of the value of the meeting or trip: "Overall, this was a productive month since we were able to complete the drawings for the major warehouse expansion. We were also able to eliminate the backlog of work that had accumulated during the warehouse project."

In minutes of meetings and trip reports, What Prompts Your Document Now often states the purposes of the meeting or trip. In that case, it is important to make clear in the Opening Statement whether the purposes were accomplished. That constitutes your Position. Even in instances in which there was no explicit purpose to be accomplished, you should still state whether the meeting or trip was successful or worthwhile, or make a comparable assessment, based on your experience or the outcomes of the activity on which you are reporting.

Once you have provided this evaluation or Position, list the highlights or Conclusions for the month, meeting, or trip—"Highlights for the month were as follows: 1) We purchased a new computer-aided design program, 2) We hired . . . ."

In the Opening Statement, you should also summarize action items that result from the activity or event, or from your evaluation. Make clear in the early paragraphs who is responsible for these next steps.

The lists of activities or events, or the actual minutes of a meeting that form the usual content of these reports constitute your Data. They document the details that substantiate your evaluation of the meeting, trip, or period of activity. Therefore, they belong in the Body of your document, where, if necessary, you can provide additional information about each highlight or action item. This Data can appear on the same page as the Opening Statement or in an attachment.

Monthly Report

Following is the Opening Statement of a monthly report. The details for each of the Conclusions are provided in an attachment.

The following is a report of activities for Marketing Communications Services for March [*What Prompts Your Document Now*].

Overall, this has been a particularly productive month, since we have provided extensive services in all the areas in which we support marketing activities [*Position*].

Activities for March include the following highlights:

1. **Trade shows**—a total of six major national shows and seven regional shows in this month alone;
2. **Meeting planning**—two major national meetings for Building Products Division plus speaker support for Concrete Products Division's regional quarterly meeting;
3. **Advertising support**—increased activity on inquiries and special projects, in line with the advertising schedules and first-quarter trade show promotions;
4. **Editorial support**—increased editorial assistance in support of product line projects for sales promotional pieces, press releases, and product promotion in the trade press [*Conclusions*].

These service areas are addressed in detail in the attachment.

Minutes of Meetings

In this example of the minutes of a meeting, the entire account is an Opening Statement.

The Quality Assurance Committee met on Thursday, April 3, to reach a consensus on steps to be taken to improve laboratory practices in the Research Department [***What Prompts Your Document Now***]. I have attached a list of the people attending.

Department staff were able to agree on the need for action and we approved specific steps to ensure more accurate and efficient practices in the Department's laboratories [***Position***].

The committee will meet again next **Friday, May 20** to review committee members' progress on completing the tasks explained below [***Action Program***].

The committee agreed that the following actions are essential to establishing proper lab procedures. Committee members have assumed responsibility for completing each task, as noted.

1. **Standard operating procedures (SOPs)** must be prepared for routine training of personnel (Gillespie and Vinson);
2. **Maintenance SOPs** must be written for all electron microscopes in the labs (Cheatham);
3. **Filing systems** must be organized for computer validation records to be kept for five years after project completion (Rich);
4. **Guidelines** must be prepared to ensure that research performed by outside contractors adheres to standard laboratory procedures (Garner) [***Action Program***].

Trip Report

Finally, we have a trip report that gives a clear assessment of the value of a conference and lists three highlights.

> On September 18 and 19 I attended the conference "Planning and Managing Corporate Networks" presented by the Bechet Group in New Orleans [**What Prompts Your Document Now**]. More than 1250 people attended, representing many of the fastest-growing and innovative multinational companies [**Importance of Subject**].
>
> The conference was informative and worthwhile, and I urge everyone in the Network Support department to attend next year's conference, which will be conducted by the Bechet Group in Guadeloupe [**Position**].
>
> I have a summary of the presentations, which I would be glad to pass on to anyone who would like an account of the topics covered at the conference [**Future Work**].
>
> Highlights of the conference were as follows.
>
> - The presentations were given by outstanding people in the field and accounts of technological developments in the coming months were informative, particularly those relating to upgrades of Norvo Network.
>
> - There was plenty of time for questions from the floor, and the presenters were available during breaks for further discussion.
>
> - The conference offered numerous opportunities for participants to network with other network specialists, which should prove beneficial in the future [**Conclusions**].

Site Report

Now that you have seen examples of a standard format for status reports, trip reports, and minutes of meetings, let's use the approach to revise a site report.

A common activity that structural engineers need to report on is the site visit, whose purpose is to monitor the progress of a construction project. Nothing about the format of the following example suggests that there is anything significant to report. The reader would have to review the report closely to discover that the visit raised two issues.

To:

From: Project Number: 129502

Subject: Structural Site Observation

This memo is to document today's site visit by myself and Frank Langella. The purpose of the visit was to observe the installation of the pump room wall reinforcing, as well as the general progress of construction. The weather was sunny, 70degF with no wind. Approximately five construction laborers, one construction manager and the resident project representative were on site.

Construction activities progressing while on site included cutting the typical reinforcing at the pipe spool penetrations. No additional reinforcing, nor the pipe spool were placed yet. I was asked by the construction manager if the #5 diagonal bars were required even if #4 bars were the typical wall reinforcing—specifically at the thick South and East walls of the pump room, and also if the diagonals were required at each mat of reinforcing. I responded by saying that the diagonal bars per the detail are required only at the inside and outside mat of each wall.

Reinforcing was being placed for the revised stair construction at the pump room, basically a rat slab foundation under the walls and stairs.

The electrical duct banks in the roadway were backfilled. Excavation for the electrical connection into the building north of the site was done to the top of the existing duct bank. It was explained that the contractor will now run the conduits from the nearby vault into the building to connect rather than tying into the spare conduit in the duct bank, since the duct bank is unexpectedly encased in concrete.

Another question was raised by the construction manager about the sloping footing at the east stem wall, north of the pump room. He is proposing to use a more traditional step footing rather than the sloped footing shown on the plans. I requested that he submit his idea on a sketch in an RFI so that I could give a formal, documented response rather than a field directive. No answer was given while on site. The construction manager said he would get it ready for my review for later today. As of the writing of this memo, I have not received the RFI.

Photos are available on the Portland server. Feel free to call if you have any questions.

Site Report—Revised

The following revision of the site report makes use of lists to guide the reader's attention. The lists naturally tell the eye that significant information will be found there. This simple change in the way the information is formatted reduces the time it will take a reader to absorb the information and decide if additional action is required.

To:

From: Project Number: 129502

Subject: Union Street Structural Site Observation

This memo documents my visit today with Frank Langella to the Union Street structural site to observe the installation of the pump room wall reinforcing, as well as the general progress of construction [***What Prompts Your Document Now***]. All construction is progressing according to plan [***Position***]. The weather was sunny, 70degF with no wind. Approximately five construction laborers, one construction manager, and the resident project representative were on site [***Essential Background***].

During the visit, the construction manager raised the following two questions [***Issues***]:

1. Are #5 diagonal bars required at the thick South and East walls of the pump room, when #4 bars are the typical wall reinforcing, and are the diagonals required at each mat of reinforcing? I responded that, according to the detail, the diagonal bars are only required at the inside and outside mat of each wall.

2. Can he use a more traditional step footing at the east stem wall, north of the pump room, rather than the sloped footing shown on the plans? I did not answer his question while on site, and asked instead that he submit his proposal on a sketch in an RFI so that I could give a formal, documented response, rather than a field directive. Although the construction manager said he would prepare the RFI for my review later today, I have not received it as of the writing of this memo.

Construction activities progressing while on site included [***Issues***]:

• Cutting the typical reinforcing at the pipe spool penetrations. Neither additional reinforcing, nor the pipe spool, had been placed yet.

• Placing of reinforcing for the revised stair construction at the pump room, consisting of a rat slab foundation under the walls and stairs.

• Backfilling the electrical duct banks in the roadway. Excavation for the electrical connection into the building north of the site was done to the top of the existing duct bank. The contractor explained that, since the duct bank is unexpectedly encased in concrete, the conduits will now be run from the nearby vault into the building to connect, rather than tying into the spare conduit in the duct bank.

Photos are available on the Portland server. Please call if you have any questions [***Action Program***].

8. Informational Writing

Sharing information is often touted as an essential component of business in the information age. But it is not enough just to share information. People in business need more than information, they need to know what the information means. They need your Conclusions and Recommendations about the information: Why is it useful? What do they need to do with it? By when?

In other words, information is most useful in business when it is presented in a manner that people can use to take action.

Therefore, virtually no communication in business should be "merely informational." And yet, so much of business communication is just information, or else looks like it's just information.

Two types of "informational" writing are frequently encountered in business.

First are e-mails and documents that look informational, but aren't—somewhere in the document, and it is usually at the end, the author has buried a point of view, or Position.

The real purpose of a communication often gets buried because people put more emphasis on the Data that supports their point of view than they do on the point of view itself. This is what we call the Mystery Story approach. The communication begins with a statement of the problem or situation that has prompted it, and then proceeds to present background information and Data, often at great length. Only at the end of the document do readers find the Conclusions and Recommendations that are the real import of the communication.

Documents written in this way begin by presenting readers with a lot of information and little indication of what it is for, or what it means. Therefore, readers are better served if your Conclusions and Recommendations appear at the beginning of the document.

A second common type of informational writing really is "just information," but shouldn't be. Documentation, plans, standards, policies, procedures, and the like fall into this category of informational writing—documents that present information that would be more useful if the document also explained what the information is, why it is important, when or how readers might need to use it, with a guide to details in the document to which readers should pay particular attention.

This chapter illustrates each of these two types of informational writing, with suggestions for improving the way the information is conveyed.

Throughout the book, we have seen other examples of documents that initially appear to be "merely informational." For more illustrations of how to transform informational writing into communications that express a point of view, see the before-and-after examples on pages 14-15, 34-42, 67-72, and 84-86.

Information That Is Not Just Information—A Compliance E-mail

Following is an e-mail to a regulatory agency. The opening paragraphs suggest that the purpose of the e-mail is to inform the agency about regulations that the agency itself is responsible for enforcing.

The actual purpose of the e-mail only becomes evident in the final paragraph, in which a point of view is presented that the agency is being asked to accept.

To: Environmental Enforcement Board
From: Timberlake Engineering
Subject: **Emergency Shower and Eyewash Water Temperature Code Requirements**

The purpose of this document is to inform the Environmental Enforcement Board of Timberlake Engineering's findings regarding water temperature requirements for emergency shower and eyewash stations for the Sacramento Enhanced Wastewater Treatment (EWT) project.

The 2008 California Plumbing Specialty Code requires tepid water to be provided for supplying emergency shower and eyewash facilities. Chapter 14, Mandatory Referenced Standards, lists ISEA Z358.1-2004 in Table 14-1 as the standard around which emergency fixtures must be designed. Tepid water is defined as 60 degrees Fahrenheit for the lower limit and 100 degrees Fahrenheit for the upper limit. Sacramento's water supply temperature is below the lower limit and must be heated to meet the tepid water temperature requirements.

In addition, the U.S. Occupational Safety and Health Administration emergency shower requirements and interpretations, 1910.151(c), also refers to the ANSI/ISEA standards for specific instruction regarding the installation and operation of emergency eyewash and shower equipment.

Timberlake Engineering's design for the EWT project includes the water heaters necessary to heat the water to an appropriate temperature for the emergency shower and eyewash facilities.

Information That Is Not Just Information: A Compliance E-mail—Revised

In the revision that follows, the e-mail's Position, or purpose, is moved to the first paragraph. The relevant regulations are then presented to justify or support the e-mail's Position.

Whereas the original version of the e-mail looked primarily like a transmittal of information, the revised e-mail uses that information to demonstrate or prove a point of view.

To: Environmental Enforcement Board ✓

From: Timberlake Engineering

Subject: EWT Design Meets Emergency Shower and Eyewash Requirements

Timberlake Engineering's design for the emergency shower and eyewash facilities in the Sacramento Enhanced Wastewater Treatment (EWT) project meets the requirements for water temperature specified by the 2008 California Plumbing Specialty Code and the U.S. Occupational Safety and Health Administration [*Position*].

Water heaters have been included in the design because the temperature of Sacramento's water supply is below the lower limit required for emergency equipment [*Essential Background*].

Requirements for water temperatures of emergency equipment are as follows [*Data*]:

1. **2008 California Plumbing Specialty Code** requires that emergency shower and eyewash facilities provide tepid water, which is defined as a lower limit of 60 degrees Fahrenheit and an upper limit of 100 degrees Fahrenheit. The standard for the design of emergency fixtures is defined in Chapter 14, Mandatory Referenced Standards, Table 14-1, lists ISEA Z358.1-2004.

2. **U.S. Occupational Safety and Health Administration** emergency shower requirements and interpretations, 1910.151(c), also refers to the ANSI/ISEA standards for the installation and operation of emergency eyewash and shower equipment.

Information that Is Not Just Information—An Executive Brief

The following brief was put together to prepare an IT Vice President at a bank to meet with Google salespeople to discuss their Enterprise Search services.

Although the brief is only two pages, the information is difficult to absorb because there is so much of it. Although the bulleted lists give the impression that there is some order to the presentation, their overall affect is a bit overwhelming. And they make it look like the document really is "just information"—a collection of everything the VP might need to know about Enterprise Search. But the document leaves it up to the VP to decipher what information is actually relevant to the meeting with Google.

If we look at the document closely, however, we find at the end a list of questions to ask the Google people. The questions suggest, furthermore, that the bank already has Enterprise Search capabilities, and a strategy. Scattered throughout the rest of the document are details about the bank's existing IT systems that will be essential knowledge for negotiating with Google.

So in reality, the document is not "just information." It communicates a point of view about Enterprise Search that would enable the VP to have a conversation about Google's services based on the bank's actual needs.

Enterprise Search at Signet Bank – IT Leadership Brief
In preparation for Google meeting about Enterprise Search

What is Enterprise Search?

- Enterprise Search takes an end user's query against an index to return relevant documents and data in a result that is intended for a worker's direct consumption.
- A company may choose to include any content within its network in Enterprise Search (file shares, intranet, application information, data, etc.)
- Enterprise Search often adds value within a company by increasing the search results relevance based on "people information" – ie, who you are, who you report to, when the information was last posted, etc. Internet web searching is typically geared by number of hits or advertising dollars.

Key Players:

Three products hit the top of Gartner's MarketScope on Enterprise Search:

- **Google Search Appliance** – Googles corporate offering for search; works best with Google applications (normally cloud hosted)
- **Microsoft Search Server** (also called FAST) – FAST was purchased by Microsoft a few years back; used internally to integrate with worker applications and people information; used externally for understanding social sentiment (are others generally saying positive or negative things about you and your brand)
- **Endeca** – A company with eCommerce background; appears to have gone into search as an extension of understanding customers.

Gartner document attached for reference highlighting key players and strengths / weaknesses of each.

Current "Search" Technologies Owned by Signet Bank:

- Microsoft SharePoint Server (2007 & 2010) – intranet, team sites, external websites.
- Microsoft Search Server / Fast 2010 – purchased for the Document Center due to the high volume of query / search development.
- Recommind (purchase in business approval stages) – targeted toward legal eDiscovery and collection.

Potential Path for Implementing "Enterprise Search" at Signet Bank:

Signet Bank could leverage its investment in Microsoft's Search Server for "enterprise search." Additional servers and software licenses would be required to expand file shares, the MySignet Intranet, and others.

Microsoft's strategy is centered on the "information worker" and takes into account who a person is, who they report to, and who they work with. Signet Bank's worker personal productivity suite – email, Office, SharePoint – are Microsoft based.

Implementing Microsoft's search strategy could incorporate these "people" characteristics in the search results.

1. **Scope / Steering Decisions:**

   - What is the scope of Enterprise Search? Scope of the implementation would directly affect the time and cost of implementation.
     - Internal – file shares (which ones – departmental, personal, etc?), MySignet Intranet, MySignet Team Sites, email, data sources, other?
     - External – Signet Bank owned websites, internet content, other?
   - Business Synergies – is there a benefit to using the same tool for worker productivity, legal, records management, etc.? Or do we continue with best of breed for each?

2. **Timing**

   - The MySignet Bank Intranet Upgrade (not scheduled, but hopefully end of 2013 – a 4-month project) is planned to be implemented with FAST as the search engine.
   - This project could lay the foundation for Enterprise Search at Signet Bank with file shares and other technology added going forward.

3. **Process**

   - Security: Data Governance & Classification – Prior to implementing an Enterprise Search initiative, a data governance policy for information regardless of platform would need to be implemented.
     - For example: Classify all information by some sort of "bucket" such as – highly confidential, confidential, open internal, open public access. Open public access might be the only information exposed through Enterprise Search tools in the beginning. At one time, Pioneer had a program with a similar approach.

4. **Technology**

   - Signet Bank has already invested in search technologies that should be able to meet (and exceed) any <u>immediate</u> needs in the Enterprise Search space. (Although additional hardware/software licenses would be required. To expand to include MySignet Intranet, approximately $40k in hw/sw would be needed. Cost to expand the fileshare would need to be researched.)

- Index Maintenance / Management – Enterprise Search tools rely on an index to present search results. These indexes often consume a large number of resources.

5. People

- Staffing – Search engines are typically not out of the box. Out of the box search results need to be monitored and tuned to increase the accuracy of the search results. A full time Search Administrator (1 or more) would be needed to implement and sustain Enterprise Searching at Signet Bank.

Potential Questions for Google:

- What is their success in deploying in company with a strong worker toolset in Microsoft (Word, Excel, etc.)?
- How does Google support customers during implementation and thereafter with support? i.e. on-site consulting, training?
- Are customers able to customize index and the result sets (ie – is there a custom development add on)?
- How does the Google search integrate with "people" context if a company uses Microsoft applications?

Information that Is Not Just Information: An Executive Brief—Revised

Look now at the version of the brief below. Notice how the information has been reorganized to give the VP in half-a-page the essential information she needs for the conversation with Google. And the rest of the document is organized to make it easy for her to find any additional details she may require. Note, in particular, how the "Additional Issues and Background Information" has been organized in descending order of importance.

Enterprise Search at Signet Bank – An IT Leadership Brief
Current Situation and Questions for Google meeting about Enterprise Search

When meeting with Google about their Enterprise Search product called Search Application [***What Prompts Your Document Now***], it should be kept in mind that Signet Bank [***Essential Background***]:

- Already owns Microsoft products that should exceed our immediate needs for Enterprise Search.
- Has not yet defined the scope of our need for Enterprise Search, and therefore how much time and resources need to be invested.

Therefore, the primary question for Google is what advantages Search Application would offer Signet Bank, given our existing investment in Microsoft products and our limited need for greater Enterprise Search capabilities [***Position***].

In particular, Google should be asked [***Issues***]:

- What search capabilities does Search Application offer that Signet Bank does not already have in our Microsoft products?

- What is Google's experience implementing Search Application in strong Microsoft environments?
- Will Signet Bank be able to customize the development of indexes and result sets?
- How is employee context integrated into Google Search in Microsoft environments?
- What training, on-site consulting, and support does Google provide during implementation and ongoing, and at what price?

This document provides the following additional background on Enterprise Search [*Issues*]:

1. Enterprise Search at Signet Bank – Current Situation and Questions
2. Current Signet Bank Enterprise Search Technologies
3. Top Enterprise Search Products
4. What is Enterprise Search?

Additional Issues and Background Information

1. Enterprise Search at Signet Bank – Current Situation and Questions

Signet Bank has already invested in Microsoft's Search Server and SharePoint Server technologies that should exceed any immediate needs for Enterprise Search.

The MySignet Bank Intranet Upgrade with Microsoft Search Server as the search engine could lay the foundation for Enterprise Search at Signet Bank with file shares and other technology added over time. MySignet Bank is a 4-month project that could be scheduled for as early as the end of 2013. Approximately $40k will be required for additional servers and software licenses. Issues that will also affect the cost of Signet Bank's Enterprise Search implementation include needs for:

- Research on the cost of expanding fileshare capabilities.
- One or more fulltime Search Administrators to implement Enterprise Search, and to monitor and refine the accuracy of search results.
- A data governance policy that classifies and determines access to information based on confidentiality, regardless of the search platform selected.

Outstanding questions include:

- What Internal and External resources should be included in Enterprise Search capabilities?
  - ◦ **Internal** – which file shares (departmental, personal, etc.), MySignet Intranet, MySignet Team Sites, email, data sources, other?
  - ◦ **External** – Signet Bank owned websites, internet content, etc.?
- Whether to use the same search tool for worker productivity, legal, records management, etc., or to provide specialized tools for different functional areas, as Signet Bank currently does?

2. Current Signet Bank Enterprise Search Technologies

Signet Bank currently uses the following search technologies:

- **Microsoft Search Server / Fast 2010** – Purchased for the Document Center due to the high volume of query / search development.

- **Microsoft SharePoint Server (2007 & 2010)** – For searching intranet, team sites, and external websites.
- **Recommind** — Targeted toward legal eDiscovery and collection. Signet Bank's purchase is in the approval stages.

A feature of Microsoft Enterprise Search products is that they take into account who is doing the search, who they report to, and who they work with. Because Signet Bank's worker productivity tools – email, Office, SharePoint – are Microsoft based, implementing Microsoft's search strategy could incorporate these "people" characteristics into the search results.

3. **Top Enterprise Search Products**

The top three products in Gartner's MarketScope on Enterprise Search are:

- **Google Search Appliance** – Works best with Google applications and is normally cloud hosted.
- **Microsoft Search Server** (aka FAST) – Can be used internally to integrate with worker applications and people information; externally for understanding what people are saying about you and your brand.
- **Endeca** – Appears to be based on Endeca's understanding of customers from their experience in eCommerce.

4. **What is Enterprise Search?**

Enterprise Search is a company-wide search capability that processes end user queries against an index to return relevant documents and data. A company may include any content within its network in Enterprise Search, such as file shares, intranet, application information, data, etc. Enterprise Search indexes often consume large numbers of resources.

Enterprise Search adds value by increasing search results' relevance based on "people information" – who you are, who you report to, when the information was last posted, etc.

Instructions for Setting Up a Project

One of the most challenging tasks in business is getting other people to do things the way you think they should be done. Everyone has their own priorities, and people may or may not take the time to do things the way you want. If you are to succeed in changing the way things get done, you have to give people a reason to change their ways, and make it easy for them to do so.

An office manager put together the following instructions on new project setup for the staff of a small engineering firm. The instructions are not complicated, and everyone will benefit from a more consistent approach to project setup. But the list includes a lot of details. Will everyone actually read and remember all the steps in the process, as well as the specific details that the office manager wants them to pay attention to?

How to Setup a New Project for a New or Existing Customer

1. **Go to the appropriate year on the server at** S:\Engineering\Projects\2013
   - Click on the Project Template, then Copy and Paste it into the sidebar. It will pop up at the bottom.
   - Rename the template, using the next number and name file from the Project Manager
   - Add to ALL Client list on the server at S:\Engineering\Projects\Active Projects\Client List 2013
2. **Scan the Signed Agreement for the project**
   - Save the Agreement to the file on the server
   - E-mail the Agreement to Fred, Sam, and Shirley
3. **Create a hanging file folder with Project Number and Name**
   - File a hardcopy of the Agreement in the physical file
4. **Add to QuickBooks as an Estimate**
   - Check the Customer Center for the Client Name
   - If the client is already in the system, add the job to the client account
   - For new customers, add New Customer and New Job—include all contact info, especially an email address in case we start e-mailing invoices to clients
5. **If a retainer check came with the Signed Agreement**
   - Create a retainer invoice under the client's Job #
   - Receive the payment in QuickBooks
   - Before depositing the check, see if other payments are also ready for deposit
6. **Add as a Budget to Bill Quick**
   - Sync Bill Quick with QuickBooks — Discuss integration settings with me
   - Select the Limit Tasks option under Project Control — Discuss with me as well
   - Under Project Management, enter Client Name, then refresh
   - Under Billing, enter the SERVICE FS (Fee Schedule), which is FS 2013.
7. **In Outlook**
   - Add any new Contact information to Public Contact Folders
   - Create an E-mail Collection folder under Public Folders/Projects/Year/Job # where everyone can drag and drop important e-mails to as they arrive

Instructions for Setting Up a Project—Revised

Although good documentation should include all the steps in a process, to be useful to end-users, it must also tell them which part of the detail they are responsible for, or is most important for them to know. Just like the documentation that comes with your cell phone, you need to give readers a "Quick Start Guide" that tells them the information they need to get started. The complete documentation provides a guide to all the features.

A Quick Start Guide for opening a new project might look something like the following memo. The document is, in effect, an Opening Statement for the detailed list of instructions above. Its purpose is to ensure that readers focus on the details that people tend to forget when setting up a new project.

How to Setup a New Project for a New or Existing Customer

In response to Jack's request in Monday's staff meeting, I have attached a checklist of all the steps for setting up a new project in our project management and financial systems [**What Prompts Your Document Now**].

A primary consequence of not following these procedures is that invoices can be delayed, which of course affects timely payment and cash flow [**Importance of Subject**].

Please review the following list of steps in the process. Each step includes a reminder about a detail that tends to be forgotten [**Position**]:

1. **Create a project file on the server** – Remember to add the project to the ALL Client list at <u>S:\Engineering\Projects\Active Projects\Client List 2013</u>

2. **Scan the Agreement and file it on the server** – And e-mail a copy of the Agreement to Fred, Sam, and Shirley.

3. **Create a Hanging File Folder** – File a copy of the Agreement in the folder.

4. **Set the project up in QuickBooks** – Please include an e-mail address, since we will probably start e-mailing invoices to clients in the next few months.

5. **Before depositing a retainer check**, ask Shirley if there are other checks that should be deposited at the same time.

6. **In Bill Quick**, talk to me if you need help syncing with QuickBooks, or with the Project Control settings.

7. **In Outlook**, create an E-mail Collection folder, in addition to entering new Contact information.

Attention to these details should reduce the frustration we all feel when project information is missing or tracking systems were not in place.

Thanks!

Software Documentation

A scientist writes a software routine that will help colleagues analyze experimental data. The following documentation explains how to use the script. The process is simple. Therefore, the following instructions may be sufficient to explain how to use the program.

Like most documentation, however, the instructions launch right into a detailed explanation of the steps the user must follow. There is no introduction that orients the reader to what they are about to learn. How easily will a first-time user be able to absorb the details of a process they are not yet familiar with? Wouldn't the detail be easier to understand if the documentation provided a simple overview of the steps before presenting the detailed instructions?

Steps to Generating Lookup Tables for Use in IEX Column Simulation

1. Store adsorption data from experiments in a .mat file
   a. Open "GenerateMATofData.m" in Matlab
   b. Alter the group of parameters under the "File Parameters" heading to match. Manually enter the data for C* and q* separated by commas; the units of the data must be in mg/mL. Be sure that the value for the SaveFile parameter has a unique string that identifies the protein and ends with "Single.mat". The unique string will be used throughout the process.
   c. Alter the group of parameters under the "Physical Parameters" heading to match the physical parameters.
   d. Run the script
   e. Repeat steps b – d until all the available data has been stored (one file for each set of adsorption data).

2. Fit the adsorption data to obtain the colloidal parameters (Keq and Bpp) as a function of ionic strength and store the interpolation functions for these parameters along with the important physical parameters in .mat files.
   a. Open "Main_Fitting_Script.m" in Matlab
   b. Alter the group of parameters under the "User Parameters" for the component to be fit.
   c. If desired, manually enter the values of the parameters for the interpolation functions under the "Set interpolation function parameters". The parameters are defined as follows: $K_{eq} = 10^{Keq\_\log A} I^{Keq\_n}$; $B_{pp} = Bpp\_b \exp\left(-Bpp\_a\sqrt{I}\right)$. If a case does not exist for the unique string that is being used, then one can be added by copying and pasting, then changing the values, or the name of one of the current cases can be changed.
   d. Run the script
   e. Repeat steps b – d for each of the two components.

3. Generate the Lookup tables
   a. Open "GenLookupTable.m" in Matlab
   b. Alter the group of parameters under the "User Parameters" heading.
   c. Run the script

Instructions for Generating Binary Plots of Data for Visualization

1. First perform steps 1 and 2 above then:
   a. Open "ViewBinaryData.m" in Matlab
   b. Enter the unique strings corresponding to the components to be evaluated.
   c. Manually enter the value of Keq and Bpp at the salt concentration of interest.
   d. Alter the remaining user parameters to match the desired output.
   e. Run the script.
   f. The plots will be saved as the name of the unique string plus the word binary (eg. CYC Binary.pdf).

Software Documentation—Revised

Wouldn't the above instructions benefit from something like the following introduction? The intention is to give readers a conceptual overview of the script and how to use it, before giving them with all the details. An introduction like this will also help to make the documentation, and therefore the software, more intelligible to users at a later point in time.

Including an introduction, or Opening Statement, with documentation is particularly important when the documentation is more than one page. When there are multiple lists of instructions and the detail is much greater, readers need an orientation that connects them with the purpose of the process or procedure that is described, and maps the details that follow.

Generating Lookup Tables and Plots for Use in IEX Column Simulation ☑

Following are instructions for running the script to generate lookup tables for use in IEX column simulation. Also included are instructions for creating binary plots of the resulting data [*What Prompts Your Document Now*].

Although the script setup is straightforward, keep the following details in mind as you become familiar with the process [*Position*, followed by *Issues*]:

- Before running the script, you will be prompted to create a separate .mat file for each set of adsorption data from your experiments. File Parameters and Physical Parameters for each file will need to be altered to match the characteristics of each data set.

- The value for the SaveFile parameter, in particular, must have a unique string that identifies the protein and ends with "Single.mat". This string will be used throughout the process.

- When fitting the adsorption data to obtain the Keq and Bpp colloidal parameters as a function of ionic strength, there are options for manually entering both the Interpolation Functions for these parameters, as well as significant Physical parameters.

- When generating the Lookup tables, parameters will again need to be altered.

The script for generating binary plots from the lookup tables follows a similar logic.

Complete instructions for the process are included below.

9. Technical Writing

THE PRIMARY DIFFERENCE BETWEEN TECHNICAL WRITING AND other forms of business writing is that the information presented is, well ... technical. In other words, the vocabulary and concepts are more specialized in nature than in "garden variety" business writing.

Apart from that difference in content, however, the objective of good technical writing is the same as in all good writing. It is to clearly communicate the Position that the technical information proves. The unique challenge of technical writing is to make that message clear even to readers who may not understand all the technical details of the material being presented. Therefore, the principles presented in *Organizing Ideas* apply with equal validity to technical writing as they do to all types of business correspondence.

To demonstrate that technical writing is most readable when it is organized according to the sequence on the *Worksheet for Organizing Ideas*, here is a three-page technical memo. Even if you don't understand the content, the structure will be clear.

More examples of technical writing can be found in Chapters 5 and 6 on reports.

TO:
FROM:
DATE:

Subject: Removal of Tetralins from Alkylate by Selective Sulfonation

The corporate Competitive Position Team has requested an evaluation of strategies for removing tetralins from alkylate. I have completed an evaluation of the selective sulfonation alternative [**What Prompts Your Document Now**].

Based on my evaluation, I recommend this option not be pursued further [*Position*] because of the following consequences of its implementation:

1. Variable cost of N-500 would increase by at least $12.6 MM per year
2. Maximum production capacity of N-500 would drop to 232 MM lb. per year
3. A 74.1 MM lb. sulfonation waste stream would be produced with a disposal cost of $5.2 MM per year
4. Production of muriatic acid would increase by 25% to 173,400 tons per year, which could result in $3.7 MM per year additional acid destruction costs [*Conclusions*].

These estimates are based on an N-500 production rate of 218 MM lb. per year projected in FY 2009 budget [*Assumptions*]. A description of the selective sulfonation process and a discussion of the above issues are presented on the attached pages.

Please forward any questions or comments to me.

Attachment

Attachment—Removal of Tetralins from Alkylate

Process Description

Since the rate of sulfonation of tetralins has been shown to be ten times greater than that for LAB (RR-816-10-3-66), it is theoretically possible to exploit this selectivity difference for the removal of tetralins from alkylate by sulfonation. However, a major drawback is the loss of monoalkylate to sulfonation.

It was shown that sulfonation with 7 lb. SO3 per 100 lb. alkylate (11% tetralins) treated would reduce the tetralin content to essentially nil and would be accompanied by a 10% loss due to sulfonation of monoalkylate. The sulfonated alkylate and tetralin would be removed from the LAB—for example, by solvent extraction or ion-exchange—to yield the tetralin-free N-500 product [*Background*].

The simplified process flow diagram for production of tetralin-free N-500 by selective sulfonation of alkylate with a similar composition to the current N-500 product which has 10% tetralins is shown below.

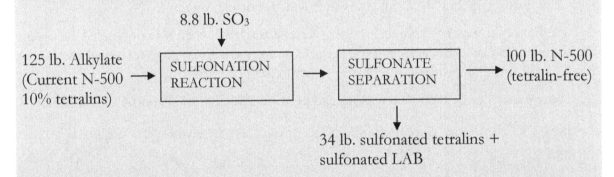

1. Increased Variable Cost of N-500

If a selective sulfonation process was placed in operation, 25% of the current N-500 would be lost due to sulfonation of the tetralin and the alkylate. In addition, significant quantities of SO_3 would need to be purchased. These factors combined increase the variable cost of N-500 production by 5.8 cents/lb. or $12.6 million per year, as shown below [*Conclusion*].

A) N-500 Yield Loss

0.25 x $0.20/lb. N-500	=	$0.05/lb. N-500
$0.05/lb. x 218 MM lb./yr.	=	$10.9 million

B) Purchase of 3540 tons of SO_3

0.0875 lb. SO_3/lb. N-500 x $0.09/lb. SO_3	=	$0.0079/lb. N-500
$0.0079 lb. x 218 MM lb. N-500/yr.	=	$1.72 million

Total　=　5.8 cents/lb. N-500　– or –　$12.6 million

2. Decreased Maximum Production Capacity of N-500

Because of the loss of alkylate and tetralin to sulfonation, the N-500 maximum production rate would be reduced from 290 MM lb. to 232 MM lb. per year. This is without the production of specialty alkylates V-7050 and V-170. The ability of this company to respond to increasing demand for N-500 would be seriously limited and specialty alkylate production would be reduced [*Conclusion*].

290 MM lb./yr. x (1.0/1.25)   =   232 MM lb. N-500/yr. capacity

3. Production and Disposal of Sulfonated Material

Removal of tetralins by selective sulfonation would result in the production of 34 lb. of sulfonated material per 100 lb. N-500 produced or 74.1 MM lb. per year. This sulfonated material could be disposed of as fuel for cement kilns at a rate of 7 cents per lb., for a total cost of $5.2 MM per year as shown below. If the material must be incinerated, the cost would double to $10.4 MM [*Conclusion*].

0.34 x 218 MM lb./yr.   =   74.1 MM lb./yr. waste stream

74.1 MM lb./yr. x $0.070 lb.   = $5.2 million

4. Increased Production of Muriatic Acid

A 25% increase in alkylate production rates to compensate for the yield loss would mean a 25% increase in muriatic acid production rates. This would increase the budgeted acid production from 138,700 tons per year to 173,400 tons per year. This would change the traditional ratio of muriatic acid produced to N-500 produced from 1.27 to 1.59 lb. muriatic acid per pound of N-500. This additional acid would need to be sold or destroyed. If it is destroyed, acid destruction costs would increase by $3.7 million per year as shown below [*Conclusion*].

1.25 x 138,700 tons/yr.   =   173,400 tons/yr.

34,700 tons/yr. x $107/ton   = $3.7 million

10. Journal Articles and Research Papers

ONE OF THE FOLLOWING TWO PASSAGES IS AN EXCERPT FROM A journal of sociology, and the other is a spoof composed by an eminent sociologist. Which is which?

> The third major component of modeling phenomena involves the utilization of symbolic representations of modeled patterns in the form of imaginal and verbal contents to guide overt performances. It is assumed that reinstatement of representational schemes provides a basis for self-instruction on how component responses must be combined and sequenced to produce new patterns of behavior.

> The purpose of this scheme is to present a taxonomic dichotomization which would allow for unilinear comparisons. In this fashion we could hope to distinguish the relevant variables which determine the functional specificities of social movements. Any classificatory scheme is, essentially, an answer to an implicit other scheme. In this instance, it is an attempt to answer the various hylozoic theories which deny that social categories can be separable.

If you find them indistinguishable, you are not alone. Is it any wonder that a prominent sociological journal found, in surveying its subscribers, that only ten readers on average managed to get all the way through any given article?

And if you happen to be a geologist, biologist, chemist, accountant, or mechanical engineer for whom all that sociological verbiage is gibberish, rest assured that your professional journals are equally unintelligible to sociologists.

Part of the problem is that journal articles and research papers are frequently written to "impress" rather than "express." The words are too big, the sentences and paragraphs too long, and the thought process too convoluted.

But not all of these problems can be blamed on authors. Journals often have strict guidelines for authors, which result in poorly structured articles. Research departments have formats that restrict the logical presentation of information.

The usual journal article or research paper has the following sections: abstract, introduction, methods, results and discussion, and conclusions. These sections contain the same ingredients we have seen on the *Worksheet for Organizing Ideas*, as shown on the next page. Keep in mind that the abstract is an Opening Statement but shorter than those that appear in most memos and letters. Therefore, you should include only essential information in this section.

Abstract—*summarizes some or all of the following items:*

- What Prompts Article/Paper Now—*recent work, scientific controversy, problem paper addresses, purpose of paper*

- Importance of Subject—*impact on particular research, new solution*

- Position—*thesis of paper, what readers should learn from the paper*

- Essential Background—*brief history of problem or prior work, context of work*

- Sources of Data—*methods, scientific approach*

- Assumptions & Limitations—*contingencies upon which Position is based*

- Major Conclusions—*central findings which substantiate the Position*

- Future Work—*the next step*

Introduction—*orients the readers by covering the following information*

- Essential Background—*expanded account of problem, prior work, scope of paper*

- Definition of Terms—*any terminology the readers must know*

Methods and Materials/Experimental Section—*establishes credibility of the paper by covering these points:*

- Sources of Data—*details on how work was performed*

- Assumptions & Limitations—*theoretical basis of work*

Results and Discussion (preferably combined into one section)—*provides substantiation for Conclusions noted in the Abstract.*

- Conclusions and supporting Data

Conclusion (may be omitted)—*reiterates key points from Abstract*

- Position—*restatement of central thesis of article/paper*

- Conclusions—*summary of key findings supporting Position*

- Future Work—*what needs to be done next*

And in case you are still wondering, the first excerpt of sociological gobbledygook at the beginning of this section appeared in a journal and was quoted by William Zinsser in his book *Writing to Learn*. The second was composed as a parody by the sociologist Daniel Bell. He sent it to three of his professional colleagues, who responded with praise and requests for prior work Bell claimed to have done in a footnote. Maybe sociologists can fool all of the people all of the time.

11. Résumés and Cover Letters

When getting ready to look for a job, composing a cover letter is not always given as much thought as preparing or updating a résumé. Yet an effective cover letter is at least as important for getting employers' attention.

In terms of the structure presented in *Organizing Ideas*, you can think of a cover letter as an Opening Statement and the résumé as the Body. But since a résumé does not actually discuss the point of view expressed in the cover letter, a truer way to think of a résumé is that it is an attachment providing Data. A very important attachment, but an attachment nonetheless.

Conceived in this way, a résumé is Data that requires a cover letter to explain its meaning or significance. The cover letter tells a story or makes an argument about who you are, what you have done, and why you are the most qualified candidate for a position. In a cover letter you tell an employer what you want them to understand about the experience that is outlined in your résumé. Without a cover letter to make your story explicit, a résumé is just Data that readers can interpret any way they choose.

Therefore, a good cover letter needs a clear and forceful Position that says you are the best candidate for a job. Your Position is supported by sound Conclusions that explain why, summarizing your qualifications as a professional. If your cover letter succeeds in gaining readers' attention, they will turn to the résumé to see in more detail how your education and experience have given you the qualifications you claim.

Your cover letter and résumé should each be limited to one page. Your objective is to make a case for yourself that is strong enough to get an interview. Then in the interview, you use your résumé as the basis for a more in depth conversation about who you are.

Ideally, the content of a cover letter should address the professional capabilities each employer is looking for. Although you may begin by composing a more generic description of your capabilities, you will want to adapt your cover letter to the specific requirements of each job for which you apply.

While the format of the résumé remains the same in the examples that follow, the order of the information depends on the circumstances of each applicant. Hence, education is the lead item in the first example of a résumé for a new MBA, whereas in the second example, experience is the selling point because the person has already spent several years in business.

A Graduate's Cover Letter and Résumé

The first example is a cover letter and résumé for a recent graduate. The résumé uses the format required by the placement office at the Harvard Business School. In particular, the placement office stipulates that the résumé must fit on one page, regardless of the experience or number of degrees a person may have.

Mr. Benjamin Pollack
Pollack Partners
711 Swing St.
Kansas City, MO 77011

Dear Mr. Pollack:

I would like to meet with you to discuss career opportunities at Pollack Partners [**What Prompts Your Document Now**]. I will graduate from Harvard Business School this June and am interested in the innovative work your firm is doing in management consulting [**Importance of Subject**].

I am confident I have a range of talents that will benefit Pollack Partners [**Position**]. Three examples follow.

- **Extensive experience with entrepreneurial ventures**—In creating and participating in a range of enterprises, from an academic research center to a textile design company, I have demonstrated my ability to set and implement strategic priorities. I have also managed relationships with a wide variety of people and entities.

- **Balance of analytical and creative skills**—My work experiences have ranged from the extremely analytical, such as the competitive cost study that I performed for Hackett Parcel Service last summer, to the very creative, such as the aesthetic decisions concerning fabric and colors I made as founder of Serpentine Textile Designs.

- **Strong project orientation**—As assistant director of the Greer Center for Leadership and Career Studies, I successfully managed numerous simultaneous projects. These efforts included field research studies, development campaigns, publicity efforts, and a conference series for executives in service industries [**Conclusions**].

I have attached my résumé to give you an account of my experience. From December 17 to 20, I will be in Kansas City and would like to meet with you to discuss the possibility of a position with Pollack Partners. I will call you next week to see if there is a time that is convenient [**Future Work**]. In the meantime, you can reach me at (617) 876-8577 [**Action Program**]. Thank you for your consideration.

Very truly yours,

William Eckstine

Attachment

WILLIAM ECKSTINE
636 Mount Auburn St.
Cambridge, MA 02138
(617) 876-8577

Education

2007 – 2009   HARVARD GRADUATE SCHOOL
OF BUSINESS ADMINISTRATION   Boston, MA
Candidate for Masters of Business Administration degree, June 2009.
General management curriculum with concentration in competitive strategy
and marketing.

2000 – 2004   HARVARD COLLEGE   Cambridge, MA
Awarded B.A. magna cum laude in Classics. Selected for departmental prize
for excellence in the Classics, Harvard College Scholarship for academic
excellence, Dean's List four semesters.

Experience

2005 – 2007   HACKETT PARCEL SERVICE   Hastings, CT
International Marketing Intern. Worked with corporate marketing to
define international strategy by structuring and performing analysis and
interpreting and presenting results to top management.
- Prepared Board of Directors review of international transportation
  services market and HPS position within market
- Conducted analysis of competitors' global air network
- Studied rate structure, zone definition, and projected profitability of
  potential service offering

2004 – 2005   GREER CENTER FOR LEADERSHIP
AND CAREER STUDIES   Macon, GA
An academic research center focusing on U.S. competitiveness

Assistant Director. Coordinated research and external relations for
Center's first year of operations.
- Managed seven MBA research assistants and a $450K annual budget
- Formulated and planned conferences on strategic challenges
- Produced $50K video series of conferences highlights

1999 – 2003   SERPENTINE TEXTILE DESIGNS   Cambridge, MA
A textile design company specializing in hand-dyed clothing

Oversaw business, from design and manufacturing to sales
- Stocked a range of exotic silks, exploring sourcing options
- Established and maintained relationships with subcontractors
- Acquired wholesale and retail clients in U.S. and U.K.

Personal

- Qualified for U.S. Triathlon Championships, 2000 – 2001
- Volunteer for Samaritan Suicide Hotline, Boston, MA

A Cover Letter for an Experienced Job Applicant

This cover letter is for a person who has business experience and seeks a new position. In such a case an attachment providing Data for each of the qualifications can be appropriate. In Attachment 1 on the next page you will see the beginnings of the Data to support each of the Conclusions that make the candidate suited for the job. In this example, the résumé is Attachment 2 which I have not shown since the résumé in the previous example is a good model.

Ms. Mabel Mercer
Director of Human Resources
Evans Incorporated
Evansville, IN 30788

Dear Ms. Mercer:

This letter responds to your advertisement for Manager of Information Services in the Chicago Gazette [***What Prompts Your Document Now***]. I am acquainted with your operation through friends who work for Evans Incorporated, including Art Farmer, and I am extremely interested in this position [***Importance of Subject***].

I believe I have four qualifications that meet the requirements set forth in your ad and make me especially suited for this job [***Position***]:

- Ten years of IT experience in planning, budget preparation and management of administrative computing, technical services, network, and operations in companies comparable to Evans Incorporated;

- Demonstrated success in handling operations-related tasks for financial reporting systems and in developing procedures for disaster recovery events;

- Proven track record in aggressive implementation/migration to new platforms;

- Familiarity with Evans Incorporated's computing environment, including extensive knowledge of Delphi and Omega databases [***Conclusions***].

Attachment 1 presents detail for each of the qualifications listed above and Attachment 2 is my one-page résumé.

I will call you on Monday to answer any questions you may have and set up a convenient time for us to meet [***Future Work***]. In the meantime, many thanks for taking the time to review this letter.

Very truly yours,

Sidney Catlett

Attachments

Attachment 1—Qualifications of Sidney Catlett

The four factors that make me qualified for the position of Manager of Information Services at Evans Incorporated are (1) ten years of IT experience in comparable companies, (2) success in handling financial reporting systems and procedures for disaster recovery; (3) proven record in aggressive implementation/migration to new platforms, and (4) my familiarity with Evans Incorporated's computing environment

Ten Years of IT Experience

Since 1995, when I completed my Masters in Computer Science, I have devoted my professional life to information services. In my current job as Director of Information Resources at Grimes Corporation, a position I have held for four years, I am responsible for. . . .

Handling Financial and Disaster Recovery Procedures

In the period 1999 to 2001, I prepared the backup and disaster recovery procedures for three major corporations while I was a consultant for the firm of Parker Associates. These procedures included such components as. . . .

Implementation/Migration to New Platforms

In my capacity as director of Information resources at Grimes, I initiated and supervised the migration of our. . . .

Familiarity with Mainframe Environment

At Grimes we have used the Delphi and Omega databases extensively in the management of our financial information and I have been responsible for staying abreast of the increasingly sophisticated features available for. . . .

12. Editing Paragraphs and Sentences

EDITING IS A SKILL THAT SOME PEOPLE SEEM TO COME BY naturally. A good editor is able to see patterns in the way words are combined to convey meaning and recognize how a different arrangement of words and phrases can more effectively communicate the same meaning. Whether or not you possess this ability has nothing to do with innate intelligence. It is a skill that some people come by in the same way that some people have a facility to see patterns in data, compose music, or create visual images. Some people simply have an "ear" for words.

Like any skill, the ability to edit can be developed. It requires paying attention, over time, to the ways that words work together, and noticing, or even just hearing, what combinations express meaning more effectively than others. Editing your own writing is particularly challenging, since it requires the ability to recognize and change patterns in the way you write that are probably as natural to you as the way you speak.

The following exercise is provided as an illustration of editing. Review the principles for editing paragraphs and sentences in *Organizing Ideas* and then read the following text out loud. Although the text is certainly understandable, you should be able to hear the unnecessary words, the long sentences, the twenty dollar words and phrases.

Take a pencil and mark changes in the text that, to your ear, would make it more readable. Then, compare your changes with the suggested edit that follows.

Procurement Methods

Revise the following text using the nine principles for editing paragraphs and sentences explained in *Organizing Ideas*.

There are several equipment procurement formats that are commonly used to purchase equipment for public works projects including an Open Bid format, Pre-Selection of Major Equipment, the Base Bid format, and Base Bid/Alternate Deduct format. Each of these formats has advantages and potential pitfalls when viewed by such diverse parties as the contractor, the equipment supplier, and the Owner/Engineer. The challenge to project owners is to utilize a procurement format that will result in the exclusion of inferior equipment while maintaining a high level of competition and participation among qualified equipment manufacturers and suppliers.

Open Bid

In the Open Bid format, the engineer specifies the attributes of the equipment to be provided and refrains from specifically naming manufacturers and models of equipment.

Conformance of the equipment to the specification is determined following award of the contract. This method of procurement encourages maximum competition as the contractor is free to shop a variety of sources for the best prices and vast arrays of suppliers are free to offer their equipment to contractors.

The problem with this type of format is that it requires the contractor to determine if the equipment meets the specification during the hectic bid process and it tends to drive contractors to select major equipment based solely on cost. These drawbacks can result in an overall lowering of the quality of the project equipment and cause conflicts arising from rejection of equipment during the submittal process for failure to meet the specification. This system also can result in "bid shopping" following award of the contract, where the bidder shops equipment suppliers to find the lowest cost items available in order to boost project profits. Bid shopping is counterproductive to the project resulting in an overall lowering of the quality of the major equipment without a corresponding reduction in project cost. The contractor, as well as the engineer, must perform additional work to ensure that the proposed equipment meets specification. The utility customer may be adversely affected if utilities are required to accept inferior equipment that will require more maintenance or earlier replacement.

Base Bid

In the Base Bid Format, the engineer specifies the attributes of the equipment to be provided, specifically naming one or more manufacturers and models of equipment that would be acceptable.

Under this format, the contractor is bound by the contract language to provide one of the "named" pieces of equipment for each category of equipment required. The equipment is normally selected based on criteria such as owner's preference for a particular operational or maintenance feature, compliance with existing equipment, recognition as an industry leader for quality or function, or because it is the only known manufacturer able to supply a particular piece of equipment deemed necessary for the success of the project.

This format is advantageous in that contractors are not required to make any assumptions prior to the bid as to which equipment meets specification, it eliminates post-bid shopping by contractors, and it ensures that the equipment provided is the type envisioned by the project designer. The project is, therefore, awarded to the contractor who can most efficiently organize and perform the project requirements at the lowest cost. The downside to this format is that it can exclude participation by suppliers who feel that their product is equal to the equipment specified.

Base Bid/Alternate Deduct

The Base Bid/Alternate Deduct format offers the benefits of the Base Bid format while including suppliers that have a new, innovative, or overlooked product. There are two basic versions of this format; the first allows for consideration of alternate deduct equipment ("or equal" equipment) prior to the award of the bid, the second allows for consideration of the alternate deduct following award of the bid.

In the former case, the owner is required to consider a wide range of potential equipment offered by the bidding contractors and make a determination as to the compliance of the equipment prior to the award of the contract. The acceptable equipment is then used to formulate a bid price and the low bidder is awarded the project. While this format offers the advantage of providing named equipment for the project as well as allowing "or equal" suppliers the chance to offer an alternative, it can be very contentious from the bidder's point of view as the winning bid is based on interpretation of the specification by the engineer or owner at bid time.

The latter version of this format allows for consideration of the alternate or "or equal" equipment following the award of the project by change order. This version of Base Bid/Alternate Deduct format offers the advantages of the Base Bid format in that the owner receives the equipment specifically named into the project design and post-bid shopping is eliminated. This method also allows a mechanism for "or equal" equipment to be considered by the owner following award of the contract when the time constraints of the bid process have been removed. However, there is minimal incentive to list alternative equipment.

Procurement Methods—Revised

Following is a revision of the preceding text on bid methods that does not show the specific changes that have been made.

Since editing is more a matter of "feel" than it is of "right answers," there are often multiple ways to improve a text. Therefore, consider the changes in the version that follows as suggestions. Compare them with your own changes. What editing choices did you make that differ from the changes below? What principle of editing were you applying in each change?

Three methods are commonly used to purchase equipment for public works projects: Open Bid, Base Bid or Pre-Selection of Major Equipment, and Base Bid/Alternate Deduct. Each method has advantages and disadvantages for contractors, equipment suppliers, and project owners and engineers.

The challenge for project owners is to use a procurement method that excludes inferior equipment while also maintaining competition between equipment manufacturers and suppliers.

Open Bid

In the Open Bid method, the project engineer specifies the attributes of the equipment to be provided, without naming manufacturers or equipment models. Whether equipment meets specifications is determined after the contract has been awarded.

This method encourages maximum competition, since contractors can shop for the best prices from equipment suppliers.

Limitations of the Open Bid method, however, are that it requires contractors to determine whether equipment meets specifications during the already hectic bid process, and it tends to encourage contractors to select equipment solely on the basis of cost. As a result, the approach can reduce the overall quality of project equipment, and create conflicts when equipment is rejected during the submittal process for failure to meet specifications.

Open Bid procurement can also result in "bid shopping," in which the winning contractor shops equipment suppliers for the lowest cost equipment to increase project profits. Bid shopping is counterproductive because it lowers the quality of equipment without reducing project costs.

The method also requires contractors and project engineers to perform additional work to ensure that the proposed equipment meets project specifications. Project owners may also be adversely affected if they are required to accept inferior equipment that will require more maintenance or earlier replacement.

Base Bid

In the Base Bid method, the project engineer specifies the attributes of the equipment to be provided, and names one or more manufacturers and equipment models that are acceptable. Under this method, contractors are bound by the contract to provide "named" equipment for each category of equipment required.

Project owners and engineers usually specify equipment on the basis of such criteria as their preference for a particular operational or maintenance feature, compatibility with existing equipment, a manufacturer's recognition for quality or function, or because a manufacturer is the only source for a piece of equipment needed for the project.

The advantages of the Base Bid method are that contractors do not have to determine which equipment meets project specifications, it eliminates bid shopping, and it ensures that the equipment provided is the type envisioned by the project owner or engineer. In this way, the project is awarded to the contractor who can most effectively deliver on the project's requirements at the lowest cost.

The downside to this method is that it can exclude participation by suppliers whose equipment is not designated in the contract, but whose products may be equal to the specified equipment.

Base Bid/Alternate Deduct

The Base Bid/Alternate Deduct method offers the benefits of the Base Bid method while also including suppliers who offer new, innovative, or otherwise overlooked products.

There are two versions of the Base Bid/Alternate Deduct method, in which alternate equipment, also referred to as "or equal" equipment, is considered either before or after the contract is awarded.

When alternate equipment is considered before awarding the contract, the project owner must evaluate equipment offered by contractors prior to bidding, and determine which equipment meets the project's specifications. Contractors then formulate a bid price for the approved equipment and the contract is awarded to the lowest bidder.

The advantages of this version of Base Bid/Alternate Deduct procurement are that it provides named equipment for the project, while also allowing "or equal" suppliers to offer alternative equipment. From the bidder's point of view, however, the process can be contentious, since the project owner or engineer must award the contract based on their interpretation of equipment specifications at bid time.

In the second version of the Base Bid/Alternate Deduct method, alternate or "or equal" equipment is considered after the contract is awarded, by means of change orders. The advantages of this approach are that the project owner receives the equipment designated in the project design, and bid shopping is eliminated.

This method also allows project owners to consider "or equal" equipment after a contract has been awarded and the time constraints of the bid process have been removed. On the other hand, the incentives for contractors to offer alternative equipment are minimal.

Procurement Methods—Revised with Mark-up

Following is a mark-up of the original text, showing all the changes that were made to arrive at the revised version above. Words that are <u>underlined</u> have been added.

Notice the number of changes that needed to be made to achieve the simple clarity of the revised text. Keep this in mind when editing someone else's writing. It may be easier for writers to accept your changes if you just give them the revised text, without showing them all your changes. Focus their attention on the effect of your edits, rather than on the details of your revision. Not everyone wants to know everything you have changed, either in Track Changes or a marked-up hardcopy.

~~There are several equipment procurement formats that~~ <u>Three methods</u> are commonly used to purchase equipment for public works projects<u>:</u> ~~including an~~ Open Bid ~~format, Pre-Selection of Major Equipment, the~~ Base Bid ~~format,~~ <u>or Pre-Selection of Major Equipment,</u> and Base Bid/Alternate Deduct ~~format~~. Each ~~of these formats~~ <u>method</u> has advantages and ~~potential pitfalls~~ <u>disadvantages for</u> ~~when viewed by~~

~~such diverse parties as the~~ <u>contractors</u>, ~~the~~ equipment <u>suppliers</u>, and ~~the~~ <u>project</u> owner<u>s</u> and ~~/~~engineer<u>s</u>.

The challenge ~~to~~ <u>for</u> project owners is to ~~utilize~~ <u>use</u> a procurement ~~format~~ <u>method</u> that ~~will result in the exclusion of~~ <u>excludes</u> inferior equipment while maintaining ~~a high level of~~ competition <u>between</u> ~~among qualified~~ equipment manufacturers and suppliers.

Open Bid

In the Open Bid ~~format~~ <u>method</u>, the <u>project</u> engineer specifies the attributes of the equipment to be provided, ~~and refrains from specifically~~ <u>without</u> naming manufacturers ~~and~~ <u>or equipment</u> models ~~of equipment~~. ~~Conformance of the~~ <u>Whether</u> equipment ~~to the~~ <u>meets</u> specification<u>s</u> is determined ~~following award of the contract~~ <u>after the contract has been awarded</u>.

This method ~~of procurement~~ encourages maximum competition, ~~as the~~ <u>since</u> contractor<u>s</u> ~~is free to~~ <u>can</u> shop ~~a variety of sources~~ for the best prices ~~and vast arrays of~~ <u>from equipment</u> suppliers~~, are free to offer their equipment to contractors~~.

~~The problem with this type of format is~~ <u>Limitations of the Open Bid method, however, are</u> that it requires ~~the~~ contractor<u>s</u> to determine <u>whether</u> ~~if the~~ equipment meets ~~the~~ specifications during the <u>already</u> hectic bid process, and it tends to ~~drive~~ <u>encourage</u> contractors to select ~~major~~ equipment ~~based~~ solely on <u>the basis of</u> cost. ~~These drawbacks can~~ <u>As a</u> result<u>, the approach can reduce</u> ~~in an~~ <u>the</u> overall ~~lowering of the~~ quality of ~~the~~ project equipment, and ~~cause~~ <u>create</u> conflicts ~~arising from rejection of~~ <u>when</u> equipment <u>is rejected</u> during the submittal process for failure to meet ~~the~~ specifications.

~~This system~~ <u>Open Bid procurement can</u> also ~~can~~ result in "bid shopping<u>,</u>" ~~following award of the contract, where~~ <u>in which</u> the ~~bidder~~ <u>winning contractor</u> shops equipment suppliers ~~to find~~ <u>for</u> the lowest cost ~~items available~~ <u>equipment</u> ~~in order~~ to ~~boost~~ <u>increase</u> project profits. Bid shopping is counterproductive ~~to the project resulting in an overall lowering of~~ <u>because it lowers</u> the quality of ~~the major~~ equipment without ~~a corresponding reduction in~~ <u>reducing</u> project cost<u>s</u>.

The <u>method also requires</u> contractor<u>s</u> ~~as well as the~~ <u>and project</u> engineer<u>s</u> ~~must~~ <u>to</u> perform additional work to ensure that the proposed equipment meets ~~the~~ <u>project</u> specifications. ~~The utility customer~~ <u>Project owners</u> may <u>also</u> be adversely affected if ~~utilities~~ <u>they</u> are required to accept inferior equipment that will require more maintenance or earlier replacement.

Base Bid

In the Base Bid ~~Format~~ <u>method</u>, the <u>project</u> engineer specifies the attributes of the equipment to be provided, ~~specifically naming~~ <u>and names</u> one or more manufacturers and <u>equipment</u> models ~~of equipment~~ that ~~would be~~ <u>are</u> acceptable. Under this ~~format~~

method, ~~the~~ contractors ~~is~~ <u>are</u> bound by the contract ~~language~~ to provide ~~one of the~~ "named" ~~pieces of~~ equipment for each category of equipment required.

~~The~~ <u>Project owners and engineers usually specify</u> equipment ~~is normally selected based~~ on <u>the basis of such</u> criteria ~~such~~ as ~~owner's~~ <u>their</u> preference for a particular operational or maintenance feature, ~~compliance~~ <u>compatibility</u> with existing equipment, <u>a</u> manufacturer's recognition ~~as an industry leader~~ for quality or function, or because ~~it~~ <u>a</u> manufacturer is the only ~~known manufacturer able to supply~~ <u>source for</u> a ~~particular~~ piece of equipment ~~deemed necessary~~ <u>needed</u> for ~~the success of~~ the project.

~~This format is advantageous in~~ <u>The advantages of the Base Bid method are</u> that contractors ~~are not required to make any assumptions prior to the bid as to~~ <u>do not have to determine</u> which equipment meets <u>project</u> specification<u>s</u>, it eliminates ~~post-~~bid shopping ~~by contractors~~, and it ensures that the equipment provided is the type envisioned by the project ~~designer~~ <u>owner or engineer</u>. <u>In this way,</u> the project is<u>,</u> ~~therefore,~~ awarded to the contractor who can most ~~efficiently~~ <u>effectively</u> ~~organize and perform~~ <u>deliver on</u> the project<u>'s</u> requirements at the lowest cost.

The downside to this ~~format~~ <u>method</u> is that it can exclude participation by suppliers <u>whose equipment is not designated in the contract, but</u> ~~who feel that their~~ <u>whose</u> product<u>s</u> ~~is~~ <u>may be</u> equal to the <u>specified</u> equipment ~~specified~~.

Base Bid/Alternate Deduct

The Base Bid/Alternate Deduct ~~format~~ <u>method</u> offers the benefits of the Base Bid ~~format~~ <u>method</u> while <u>also</u> including suppliers ~~that~~ <u>who</u> ~~have a~~ <u>offer</u> new, innovative, or <u>otherwise</u> overlooked product<u>s</u>.

There are two ~~basic~~ versions of ~~this format;~~ <u>the Base Bid/Alternate Deduct method in which</u> ~~the first allows for consideration of~~ alternate ~~deduct~~ equipment, <u>(</u>also referred to as "or equal" equipment~~)~~, <u>is considered either before or after the contract is awarded.</u> ~~prior to the award of the bid, the second allows for consideration of the alternate deduct following award of the bid.~~

~~In the former case~~ <u>When alternate equipment is considered before awarding the contract</u>, the <u>project</u> owner ~~is required to consider a wide range of potential~~ <u>must evaluate</u> equipment offered by ~~the bidding~~ contractors <u>prior to bidding,</u> and ~~make a determination as to the compliance of the~~ <u>determine which</u> equipment <u>meets the</u> project's specifications ~~prior to the award of the contract. The acceptable equipment is then used to~~ <u>Contractors then</u> formulate a bid price <u>for the approved equipment</u> and the <u>contract is awarded to the</u> low<u>est</u> bidder ~~is awarded the project~~.

~~While this format offers~~ <u>The</u> advantage<u>s</u> of <u>this version of Base Bid/Alternate Deduct procurement are that it</u> ~~providing~~ <u>provides</u> named equipment for the project<u>,</u> ~~as well as~~ <u>while also</u> allowing "or equal" suppliers ~~the chance~~ to offer ~~an~~ alternative equipment. <u>From the bidder's point of view, however,</u> ~~it~~ <u>the process</u> can be ~~very~~

contentious, ~~from the bidder's point of view as~~ since the project owner or engineer must award the contract ~~the winning bid is~~ based on their interpretation of ~~the~~ equipment specifications ~~by the engineer or owner~~ at bid time.

In the ~~latter~~ second version of ~~this format~~ the Base Bid/Alternate Deduct method, ~~allows for consideration of the~~ alternate or "or equal" equipment is considered ~~following the award of the project~~ after the contract is awarded, by means of change orders. ~~This version of Base Bid/Alternate Deduct format offers the advantages of the Base Bid format in~~ The advantages of this approach are that the project owner receives the equipment ~~specifically named into~~ designated in the project design, and ~~post-bid~~ bid shopping is eliminated.

This method also allows ~~a mechanism for~~ project owners to consider "or equal" equipment ~~to be considered by the owner following award of the contract~~ after a contract has been awarded ~~when~~ and the time constraints of the bid process have been removed. ~~However~~ On the other hand, ~~there is minimal~~ the incentives for contractors to ~~list~~ offer alternative equipment are minimal.

13. Blank Worksheets

ON THE PAGES THAT FOLLOW ARE THE *Worksheet for Organizing Ideas* in its Short and Long versions, the *E-mail Outline*, the *Reader Profile Form*, and the *Worksheet for Organizing Presentations*. How to use these forms is explained in *Organizing Ideas*, the *Spence & Company* book on the principles of effective business communication. You are welcome to make copies of these forms to plan your documents and presentations.

Keep copies of the *E-mail Outline* and the *Worksheets for Organizing Ideas* and *Presentations* handy for planning your correspondence and presentations. The more you use these forms, the more quickly you will develop the habit of using their structure to organize your thoughts under any circumstance.

Consider filling out a *Reader Profile Form* when you have several key readers or are writing about a topic that requires careful thought about your readers' concerns. Use the *Reader Profile Form* when preparing a presentation, as well, to evaluate your audience's interests and concerns. For routine emails or memos, however, two minutes of thinking about your readers will probably be sufficient to make you aware of their needs.

WORKSHEET FOR ORGANIZING IDEAS—*Short Form*

SUBJECT: _____

OPENING STATEMENT or ONE-PAGE DOCUMENT

__1__ **I. Significance to the Readers**

    A. What Prompts Your Document Now? _____

    _____

    B. Importance of Subject: _____

    _____

__2__ **II. Position:** _____

    _____

____ **A. Essential Background:** _____

    _____

____ **B. Definition of Terms:** _____

    _____

    III. Methodology (if necessary)

____ **A. Sources of Data:** _____

    _____

____ **B. Assumptions & Limitations:** _____

    _____

    IV. Issues and Conclusions

____ **PRO**   ____ **CON**

    1. _____   **1.** _____

    2. _____   **2.** _____

    3. _____   **3.** _____

    4. _____   **4.** _____

    5. _____   **5.** _____

    V. Recommendations

____ **A. Action Program:** _____

    _____

____ **B. Future Work:** _____

    _____

↑   *What is the best order in which to present your information?*

WORKSHEET FOR ORGANIZING IDEAS—*Short Form*

SUBJECT: _____

OPENING STATEMENT or ONE-PAGE DOCUMENT

__1__ **I. Significance to the Readers**

    A. What Prompts Your Document Now? _____

    _____

    B. Importance of Subject: _____

    _____

__2__ **II. Position:** _____

    _____

____ **A. Essential Background:** _____

    _____

____ **B. Definition of Terms:** _____

    _____

III. Methodology (if necessary)

____ **A. Sources of Data:** _____

    _____

____ **B. Assumptions & Limitations:** _____

    _____

IV. Issues and Conclusions

____ **PRO**	____ **CON**
1. _____	1. _____
2. _____	2. _____
3. _____	3. _____
4. _____	4. _____
5. _____	5. _____

V. Recommendations

____ **A. Action Program:** _____

    _____

____ **B. Future Work:** _____

    _____

↑ *What is the best order in which to present your information?*

    ww.spenceandco.com

OUTLINE *for* E-MAIL *and* TEXTING

Subject: _____

What prompts your e-mail or text? _____

_____

What do you want your reader to do or believe? _____

_____

Why? What are your reasons or points? _____

_____

What's next? Who will do what, when, and how? _____

_____

www.spenceandco.com

. . . .

OUTLINE *for* E-MAIL *and* TEXTING

Subject: _____

What prompts your e-mail or text? _____

_____

What do you want your reader to do or believe? _____

_____

Why? What are your reasons or points? _____

_____

What's next? Who will do what, when, and how? _____

_____

ww.spenceandco.com

OUTLINE *for* E-MAIL *and* TEXTING

Subject: _____

What prompts your e-mail or text? _____

_____

What do you want your reader to do or believe? _____

_____

Why? What are your reasons or points? _____

_____

What's next? Who will do what, when, and how? _____

_____

www.spenceandco.com

....

OUTLINE *for* E-MAIL *and* TEXTING

Subject: _____

What prompts your e-mail or text? _____

_____

What do you want your reader to do or believe? _____

_____

Why? What are your reasons or points? _____

_____

What's next? Who will do what, when, and how? _____

_____

ww.spenceandco.com

READER PROFILE FORM

What is the best form of communication (e-mail, attachment, report, proposal, presentation, phone call, meeting)? _____

What do you want your readers to do or believe? _____

_____

I. Who are your key readers or decision-makers?

1. _____   3. _____

2. _____   4. _____

What do you know about your key readers?

How much do they know about you and your topic? How much detail do they want? What is their point of view about your topic? What are their core values and beliefs?

Key reader 1

- _____   - _____

- _____   - _____

Key reader 2

- _____   - _____

- _____   - _____

Key reader 3

- _____   - _____

- _____   - _____

Key reader 4

- _____   - _____

- _____   - _____

II. Who are your secondary or informational readers?

1. _____   3. _____

2. _____   4. _____

What needs and concerns do your secondary readers have?

1. _____

2. _____

3. _____

4. _____

How will your document address your readers' needs?

III. What questions will readers ask about your proposal that your document must answer?

1. _____
   _____

2. _____
   _____

3. _____
   _____

4. _____
   _____

5. _____
   _____

IV. What obstacles do you anticipate? _____

_____

_____

_____

What can you do about them? _____

_____

_____

_____

_____

_____

V. How will you inspire readers to act on your point of view? _____

_____

_____

_____

VI. How will readers use your document and how can you make it easier to use? _____

_____

_____

_____

READER PROFILE FORM

What is the best form of communication (e-mail, attachment, report, proposal, presentation, phone call, meeting)? _____

What do you want your readers to do or believe? _____

_____

I. Who are your key readers or decision-makers?

1. _____   3. _____

2. _____   4. _____

What do you know about your key readers?

How much do they know about you and your topic? How much detail do they want? What is their point of view about your topic? What are their core values and beliefs?

Key reader 1

- _____   • _____
- _____   • _____

Key reader 2

- _____   • _____
- _____   • _____

Key reader 3

- _____   • _____
- _____   • _____

Key reader 4

- _____   • _____
- _____   • _____

II. Who are your secondary or informational readers?

1. _____   3. _____

2. _____   4. _____

What needs and concerns do your secondary readers have?

1. _____

2. _____

3. _____

4. _____

How will your document address your readers' needs?

III. What questions will readers ask about your proposal that your document must answer?

1. _____

_____

2. _____

_____

3. _____

_____

4. _____

_____

5. _____

_____

IV. What obstacles do you anticipate? _____

_____

_____

_____

What can you do about them? _____

_____

_____

_____

_____

V. How will you inspire readers to act on your point of view? _____

_____

_____

VI. How will readers use your document and how can you make it easier to use? _____

_____

_____

_____

WORKSHEET FOR ORGANIZING IDEAS—*Long Form*

SUBJECT: _____

OPENING STATEMENT—*What information do you need to include?*

_1_ **I. Significance to the Readers**

    A. What Prompts Your Document Now? _____

    _____

    B. Importance of Subject: _____

    _____

_2_ **II. Position:** _____

    _____

____ **A. Essential Background:** _____

    _____

____ **B. Definition of Terms:** _____

    _____

III. Methodology (if necessary)

____ **A. Sources of Data:** _____

    _____

____ **B. Assumptions & Limitations:** _____

    _____

IV. Issues and Conclusions

____ PRO	**____ CON**
1. _____	1. _____
2. _____	2. _____
3. _____	3. _____
4. _____	4. _____
5. _____	5. _____

V. Recommendations

____ **A. Action Program:** _____

    _____

____ **B. Future Work:** _____

    _____

↑ *What is the best order in which to present your information?*

3. Issue /Conclusion /Recommendation 3

A. Identification of Issue /Conclusion /Recommendation _____
_____

   a. Background (if necessary): _____
_____

   b. Importance (if necessary): _____
_____

B. Presentation of Data

   a. _____
_____

   b. _____
_____

C. Conclusion for Issue /Recommendation: _____
_____

4. Issue /Conclusion /Recommendation 4

A. Identification of Issue /Conclusion /Recommendation _____
_____

   a. Background (if necessary): _____
_____

   b. Importance (if necessary): _____
_____

B. Presentation of Data

   a. _____
_____

   b. _____
_____

C. Conclusion for Issue /Recommendation: _____
_____

3. Issue / Conclusion / Recommendation 3

A. Identification of Issue / Conclusion / Recommendation _____

_____

    a. Background (if necessary): _____

    _____

    b. Importance (if necessary): _____

    _____

B. Presentation of Data

    a. _____

    _____

    b. _____

    _____

C. Conclusion for Issue / Recommendation: _____

_____

4. Issue / Conclusion / Recommendation 4

A. Identification of Issue / Conclusion / Recommendation _____

_____

    a. Background (if necessary): _____

    _____

    b. Importance (if necessary): _____

    _____

B. Presentation of Data

    a. _____

    _____

    b. _____

    _____

C. Conclusion for Issue / Recommendation: _____

_____

5. Issue / Conclusion / Recommendation 5

A. Identification of Issue / Conclusion / Recommendation _____

_____

a. Background (if necessary): _____

_____

b. Importance (if necessary): _____

_____

B. Presentation of Data

a. _____

_____

b. _____

_____

C. Conclusion for Issue / Recommendation: _____

_____

SUMMING UP

I. Restatement of Position: _____

_____

II. Recap of Major Conclusions

1. _____

_____

2. _____

_____

3. _____

_____

4. _____

_____

5. _____

_____

III. Recap of Recommendations

A. Action Program: _____

_____

B. Future Work: _____

_____

WORKSHEET FOR ORGANIZING IDEAS—Long Form

SUBJECT: _____

OPENING STATEMENT —*What information do you need to include?*

1 **I. Significance to the Readers**

    A. What Prompts Your Document Now? _____

_____

    B. Importance of Subject: _____

_____

2 **II. Position:** _____

_____

___   **A. Essential Background:** _____

_____

___   **B. Definition of Terms:** _____

_____

III. Methodology (if necessary)

___   **A. Sources of Data:** _____

_____

___   **B. Assumptions & Limitations:** _____

_____

IV. Issues and Conclusions

___ **PRO**	**___** **CON**
1. _____	1. _____
2. _____	2. _____
3. _____	3. _____
4. _____	4. _____
5. _____	5. _____

V. Recommendations

___   **A. Action Program:** _____

_____

___   **B. Future Work:** _____

_____

What is the best order in which to present your information?

     www.spenceandco.com

1. Issue /Conclusion /Recommendation 1

A. Identification of Issue /Conclusion /Recommendation _____

_____

   a. Background (if necessary): _____

   _____

   b. Importance (if necessary): _____

   _____

B. Presentation of Data

   a. _____

   _____

   b. _____

   _____

C. Conclusion for Issue /Recommendation: _____

_____

2. Issue /Conclusion /Recommendation 2

A. Identification of Issue /Conclusion /Recommendation _____

_____

   a. Background (if necessary): _____

   _____

   b. Importance (if necessary): _____

   _____

B. Presentation of Data

   a. _____

   _____

   b. _____

   _____

C. Conclusion for Issue /Recommendation: _____

_____

3. Issue /Conclusion /Recommendation 3

A. Identification of Issue /Conclusion /Recommendation _____

_____

   a. Background (if necessary): _____

_____

   b. Importance (if necessary): _____

_____

B. Presentation of Data

   a. _____

_____

   b. _____

_____

C. Conclusion for Issue /Recommendation: _____

_____

4. Issue /Conclusion /Recommendation 4

A. Identification of Issue /Conclusion /Recommendation _____

_____

   a. Background (if necessary): _____

_____

   b. Importance (if necessary): _____

_____

B. Presentation of Data

   a. _____

_____

   b. _____

_____

C. Conclusion for Issue /Recommendation: _____

_____

5. Issue / Conclusion / Recommendation 5

A. Identification of Issue / Conclusion / Recommendation _____

_____

   a. Background (if necessary): _____

_____

   b. Importance (if necessary): _____

_____

B. Presentation of Data

   a. _____

_____

   b. _____

_____

C. Conclusion for Issue / Recommendation: _____

_____

SUMMING UP

I. Restatement of Position: _____

_____

II. Recap of Major Conclusions

   1. _____

_____

   2. _____

_____

   3. _____

_____

   4. _____

_____

   5. _____

_____

III. Recap of Recommendations

A. Action Program: _____

_____

B. Future Work: _____

_____

WORKSHEET FOR ORGANIZING PRESENTATIONS

TITLE: _____

_____

_____

_____

_____

_____

OPENING STATEMENT

Why are we here? / Opener _____

_____

_____

_____

_____

_____

_____

Why is it important? _____

_____

_____

_____

_____

_____

What is the agenda? _____

_____

_____

_____

_____

_____

_____

Position

____ **What do you want your listeners to do or believe?**

_____

_____

_____

_____

_____

_____

____ **Essential Background:** _____

_____

_____

_____

_____

_____

_____

_____

____ _____

_____

_____

_____

_____

_____

_____

_____

____ **Definition of Terms:** _____

_____

_____

_____

_____

_____

_____

Methodology (if necessary)

___ **Sources of Data:** _____

_____

_____

_____

_____

_____

_____

___ _____

_____

_____

_____

_____

_____

___ **Assumptions & Limitations:** _____

_____

_____

_____

_____

_____

_____

___ _____

_____

_____

_____

_____

_____

BODY — Issues and Conclusions

Opening Summary of Issues and Conclusions: _____

_____

_____

_____

_____

_____

_____

_____

1. _____

_____

_____

_____

_____

_____

_____

_____

2. _____

_____

_____

_____

_____

_____

_____

_____

3. _____

_____

_____

_____

_____

_____

_____

_____

BODY — Issues and Conclusions (*Continued*)

4. _____

_____

_____

_____

_____

_____

_____

5. _____

_____

_____

_____

_____

_____

_____

___ **Closing Summary of Issues and Conclusions:** ___

_____

_____

_____

_____

_____

_____

___ ___ _____

_____

_____

_____

_____

_____

BODY — Issues and Conclusions (*Continued*)

SUMMING UP – Recommendations

____ **What do you want your listeners to do next?** ____

_____

_____

_____

_____

_____

_____

_____

____ _____

_____

_____

_____

_____

_____

_____

____ **What will you do next?** _____

_____

_____

_____

_____

_____

_____

_____

____ **Motivation / Inspiration / Closing** _____

_____

_____

_____

_____

_____

_____

_____

Made in the USA
Middletown, DE
20 April 2019